50 Bible Dramas for Children

By the same author

50 Stories for Special Occasions

50 Five-Minute Stories

50 Life-Building Stories

The Brownie Guide Book

Love Breaks Through

Jessica Joins the Brownies

Tracy and the Warriors

A Friend for Life

Failure is Never Final

Emily's Challenge

50 Bible Dramas for Children

Lynda Neilands

Eastbourne

First published 2005

ISBN 1 84291 253 4

Designed by pinnaclecreative.co.uk

Published by
Kingsway Communications Ltd
Lottbridge Drove, Eastbourne BN23 6NT, England.
Email: childrensministry@kingsway.co.uk

Printed in the USA

To the members of
'Junction' youth group

CONTENTS

PART 3: STAR PART *(From the Manger to the Throne)*

PART 4: JOIN THE COMPANY *(And Change the World)*

ACKNOWLEDGEMENTS

Some of the scripts in ***50 Bible Dramas for Children*** have been adapted from scripts written for two other drama projects. Audio versions of 'The Cheat' and 'No-Brain Noah' appear in a CD of dramatised Bible stories ***The Hullabaloo Crew*** produced by Scripture Union NI in partnership with the Boys' Brigade.

'We're Moving', 'What a Laugh', 'A Two-Way Promise', 'Quick Fix', 'Rachel's Wedding', 'Dream On', 'The Stranger' and 'Sit, Crouch, Stand' have been adapted from scripts produced for the Girls' Brigade Scripture Course ***My Chosen People.***

The drama *'On the Run'* is an expanded version of a drama which originally appeared in ***Theme Drama*** (2000 Scripture Union). I am grateful for permission to include it here.

And finally, a big 'thank you' to the men in my life – David, Christopher and Patrick. As ever, your support and encouragement has meant more than I can say.

INTRODUCTION

Drama is a bit like athletics or any other sport. You shouldn't start into it cold. It's important to warm up – limbs, facial muscles and of course vocal chords. So here's a little vocal exercise as lead-in to these drama scripts. Take a short but meaningful sentence such as 'I eat my peas with honey' and repeat it six times emphasising a different word each time. Ideally try to do this in chorus with at least six other people, allowing the final 'I eat my peas with ***honey'*** to crescendo to an enthusiastic climax. Excellent! You are now ready to read on.

We are going to do a similar exercise with the title of this book: **50 Bible Dramas for Children**. I'd like to emphasise four of the five words in this title: Bible, Dramas, For and Children.

BIBLE DRAMAS FOR CHILDREN

This is a book of ***Bible*** dramas for children because the dramas do not stand alone. They have been written as a tool for those seeking to present Bible teaching and truth – particularly those seeking to present it to children and young people. This book is a small response to a massive challenge. How do we encourage the sophisticated, emotionally charged, brand-oriented, freewheeling, screen-addicted, identity-seeking youngsters of today to engage with the Bible? Most aren't drawn to Bible study. Many never read books. Fun, choice, relationships, action, adventure… these are the things they look for in a church-based programme, and obviously these are things leaders must aim to provide. But what of the Bible content of that programme? The God we are called to reflect believes in Bible content – otherwise why would He have provided us with a unique, complex, mind-stretching written word? He's given us his Word and told us to teach it to our children. Somehow, along with the emphasis on fun, adventure, relationship-building etc, we need to find ways of unpacking the Bible and exploring the riches it contains.

BIBLE *DRAMAS* FOR CHILDREN

One way of unpacking Bible truth is through drama. This certainly isn't a new idea. God often told the prophets to act out their message. Choral singing and the reciting of psalms were part of biblical faith. In his ministry, Jesus used dramatic action as well as words. I believe one reason we have this biblical endorsement of drama as a teaching tool is because drama is effective.

Drama is effective because **engaging attention** is essential to any form of communication. No message can get through if the receivers are slumped back in their seats, eyes glazed, thoughts focused on anything other than the words that are being spoken at the front of the hall or church. Drama engages attention. It will make people sit up and listen. OK, maybe it won't make your super-cool 8-going-on-18-year-olds sit up (especially if they can appear laid back and still see) but, at the very least, we can say it's likely to arouse their curiosity and gain a hearing.

Drama is also effective in **establishing connections.** The Bible was written more than two thousand years ago by people in a very different cultural setting. The truth that it contains is still totally relevant to life today, but children and young people need to be shown how. A piece of drama can act as a bridge from their world into the world of the Bible. It can bridge the gap by presenting elements of Bible truth from their cultural standpoint, helping them see parallels between the experience of Bible characters and their own. For those who may already feel they know all there is to know about a particular Bible story or Bible character, it may throw fresh light on a familiar tale.

Last, but by no means least, drama is effective in **exploring relationships** and **encouraging personal/group development.** Through drama, spectators and participants are invited to 'feel with' characters in their relationships with one another and with God. They can safely explore conflict situations in a 'virtual reality' setting. What they learn may then be applied to real life. Similarly, the experience of taking part in drama can be very beneficial – strengthening relationships between cast members, building a sense of group identity through team-work and giving individuals a chance to 'shine'.

BIBLE DRAMAS *FOR* CHILDREN

Each of the dramas in this book has been written for use with children. This does not mean that they are all designed to be performed by children. Many of them have indeed been written for children to act out, but others will work better when they are performed by adults for the children, or with a mixture of adults and children taking part. The drama notes at the beginning indicate the level of acting ability required and whether ideally children, adults or both should perform a given script.

BIBLE DRAMAS FOR *CHILDREN*

These scripts are designed for use with children and young people up to the age of 13. This is a wide age-range. Some of the dramas are more suitable for those at the older end of the scale. Others will work better with 6–10s. The suggested age-range is indicated at the beginning of each drama. Those who wish to think more deeply about using drama activities with a particular age-range will find lots of helpful ideas in Ruth Alliston's ***Children's Ministry Guide to Dance and Drama,*** published by Children's Ministry.

Each drama is meant to be used illustratively as part of a talk or in a small group study/discussion and each should be accompanied by the Bible reading on which it is based. Sometimes the drama may be used to introduce the Bible reading; in other cases the Bible passage should be read first. With this in mind I have tried to keep the passages brief enough to be read in full (preferably from a youth-friendly version of the Bible). Where a longer passage has been chosen, the reader should feel free to summarize it in part.

How the dramas are presented will depend on the situation. In a small group setting, they could simply be read aloud. Where they are part of a talk being given to a larger group in a church or club, they may be performed by the youngsters, or as mentioned above, for the young people by adult leaders.

Because children tend to have a limited attention span, the scripts are short (most lasting 6–8 minutes). A limited number of actors is required (generally no more than 6, though often allowing scope for additional cast members). They require few props and very little scenery. If they are to be performed in public some rehearsal will be necessary, but they ought to be do-able with the minimum of fuss.

Finally each drama is followed up with an application section under the headings **explore, chat** and **think.** If the drama is to be used illustratively as part of a 'talking' slot, this section is designed to help speakers set the passage in context and identify a central teaching point.

The 'setting in context' **explore** ideas will usually contain references to other passages of Scripture. In a small group, where possible, it is good to encourage youngsters to look up these references for themselves. The ability to find a Bible book, chapter and verse is an important 'exploring' skill. The **chat** ideas should then be seen as discussion starters and the **think** ideas as a lead-in to more personal sharing and/or prayer.

Overall my hope is that in this book speakers and group leaders may find something that will strike a chord and inspire their own creativity. I do not really eat my peas with honey. I do believe that with commitment and imagination we can find ways to encourage young people to taste the honey of God's Word.

PART ONE

CURTAIN UP
(From Eden to Egypt)

DRAMA 1

ADAM AND THE GREATER SPOTTED DONKEY

AGE 8+

SUBJECT: Creation

BIBLE READING: Genesis 2:15–24

DRAMA NOTES: Suitable to be read in a small group or for performance, particularly in an all age setting, where it requires five confident actors (adults or children).

Cast: Angel, dog, owl, monkey, donkey.
Staging: The action opens with an angel standing guard outside a door leading into a walled part of the Garden of Eden. This may be indicated by a row of chairs or two screens, with a gap in the middle to represent the door.
Props: Notice saying **WANTED – JOBSHARE PARTNER** propped up on one of the chairs.

(sound of barking off stage. Angel is sitting on chair beside the gap)
Angel: Oh dear! Here comes a noisy, spotty creature. Time to do my duty. ***(stands in front of gap)***

Dog: ***(enters running and barking)*** Adam… woof… Adam… woof… woof… woof.

Angel: Shhhh! Stop barking. Adam's asleep and I'm guarding this doorway to stop him being disturbed.

Dog: ***(whining)*** Please Angel, I need to speak to him. I got a problem.

Angel: Don't be silly. You can't have a problem. This is the Garden of Eden. Everything is perfect.

Dog: I got a question then. I got a question and Adam knows the answer. ***(tries to get past Angel)***

Angel: ***(holds him back)*** Listen, Adam has spent the whole day naming animals and now he's sleeping. Tell me your question. I promise I'll ask Adam the minute he wakes up.

Dog: Oh, all right. ***(sits down mournfully)*** My question is, 'What am I?' Adam wrote my name out on a piece of card… only I lost it and now I can't remember what I am…

Angel: On a piece of card, eh. ***(stoops down, picks a card off the ground and waves it under the dog's nose)*** Would this be it?

Dog: ***(excitedly)*** Yes… yes… ***(looks up expectantly)***

Angel: ***(reads card)*** Congratulations. You're a donkey.

Dog: A donkey! ***(barks excitedly)*** Woof… woof… hurrah! ***(jumps round excitedly)*** I'm a donkey… I'm a donkey…

Angel: Shhhh. No barking…

(sound of loud twooing and squeaking off stage)

Angel: Oh no! More noise.

(enter owl and mouse twoo-ing and squeaking)

Mouse: Adam… squeak, squeak… Adam…

Owl: Adam… twit twoo… Adam… twit twoo…

Angel: ***(shouting)*** Will you lot KEEP QUIET… Adam's trying to sleep.

Mouse: But I really need to ***squeak*** to him.

Owl: Me twooo.

Angel: ***(wearily)*** Let me guess. Adam wrote your names out for you on cards and now you've lost them and you can't remember what you are.

Owl: Certainly not. I didn't need a card. I know perfectly well what I am.

Angel: Great! So why are you here?

Owl: I'm here because this silly little squeaking creature… ***(pecks at mouse)***

Mouse: Ow… stop pecking.

Owl: …is trying to steal my name.

Mouse: Adam said I was a donkey.

Owl: Correction! ***I'm*** the donkey.

Dog: ***(producing card with a flourish)*** No way. You two night creatures was sleeping when the names was called out. The only donkey round these parts is ME.

(they all keep loudly insisting that they are donkeys)

Angel: Please… please… keep quiet all of you. We really don't want to wake Adam. He's had a disappointing day…

Dog, Owl and Mouse: Disappointing? How do you mean… disappointing?

Angel: The fact is Adam feels lonely. He needs a partner, and out of all the thousands of creatures he named today, he didn't find a single one that matched the job description.

Owl: Which was?

Angel: ***(points to notice)*** Wanted – imaginative, intelligent partner to share Adam's work and be his equal in every way.

Dog: ***(eagerly)*** Yeh, sweet! You tell him there's a donkey out here who's just great at digging. ***(starts digging like a dog)*** This donkey could share Adam's work all right. Plants, flowers – I'll dig them all up.

Owl: ***(pushes him over)*** But you're not a donkey. ***I*** am.

Mouse: ***(tantrum style)*** No it's me... me... ME... I'm the donkey... I'm the donkey...
(the sound of soft romantic music, e.g. Love Changes Everything, stops the argument)

Dog: Hey, do you dig that? Music – coming from the other side of the wall.

Angel: What's going on? ***(bends over as if peering through a key hole in door – music gets louder)*** Wow! This is amazing!
(owl flies onto chair and looks over the top of the wall)

Owl: There are twoo of them. Twoo humans. God's given Adam a partner.

Dog: What sort of partner? Can it dig? Does it have spots?

Owl: It certainly doesn't have spots. And it doesn't have feathers or whiskers either. It looks the same as Adam... only different...

Angel: It's the loveliest creature I've ever seen... different, but Adam's equal in every way.

Mouse: ***(impatiently)*** He's awake then?

Angel: ***(turns round in surprise)*** Of course he's awake.

Mouse: ***(moving towards door, beckoning to dog and owl)*** So what are we waiting for? Come on. The humans are ready to look after us.

Angel: No, wait. I'm sure they'd rather be alone for a little longer. ***(music fades but continues softly in the background)*** Look! How's this for an idea? ***(points to dog)*** You could be a greater spotted donkey. ***(points to mouse)*** You could be a lesser whiskered donkey. ***(points to owl)*** And you could be a flying, tufted donkey.

(enter donkey N.B. Donkey plays part solemnly and mournfully until the last line)
Donkey: Excuse me... sorry for interrupting... but would you have a name for a creature like me? I dropped my card, you see. All I remember is that the second letter was an 'o'.

Dog, Owl and Mouse: You are ***not*** a donkey.

Donkey: Notadonkey? Are you sure? Notadonkey seems a very strange name. I rather think I should check that out with Adam.

Angel: OK... right.... I've had enough. ***(mimes throwing open door and stands back)*** On you go...
(animals exit noisily through gap shouting things like 'Come on then' and 'The humans will sort us out'. Music stops)

Angel: ***(looks through the door after them, then turns back and sits on seat)*** Well, the honeymoon is over. But at least there are two of them to sort those creatures out. Adam has the helper he needs.

(mouse, dog and owl come running back through gap and across the stage in front of the angel shouting excitedly)
Mouse: I'm a mouse.

Owl: I'm an owl.

Dog: I'm a dog.

(donkey follows them slowly through gap and stops to speak to angel)

Donkey: ***(solemnly)*** Well, I spoke to Adam's wife and she told me I was very clever to realise that Notadonkey wasn't my real name.

Angel: So what ***is*** your real name?

Donkey: It's Youradonkey.

Angel: Youradonkey!

Donkey: That's what she said. Youradonkey. A yippedy-do-da Youradonkey – that's me!

APPLICATION

Theme: God's design in creation

Explore: Genesis

The word Genesis means ***beginnings*** or ***origins.*** The book of Genesis is the first book in the Bible. It gives us a way of looking at life and making sense of what we see. It answers big questions. Where did the universe come from? (Genesis 1:1–26) What are human beings meant to do? (Genesis 1:28) What went wrong? (Genesis 3:1–17) How is it to be put right? (Genesis 3:15).

Chat

Watch a wildlife programme or video. Talk about things in nature that make you think of God. Christians may have different views on how God created the world (you may want to chat about this), but the Bible clearly tells us that creation happened according to His plan.

Think

The Lord God said, 'It is not good for the man to be alone. I will make a helper suitable for him.' (Genesis 2:18) Pray for people who are lonely or struggling – that God will send the companions and the help they need.

DRAMA 2

THE BLAME GAME

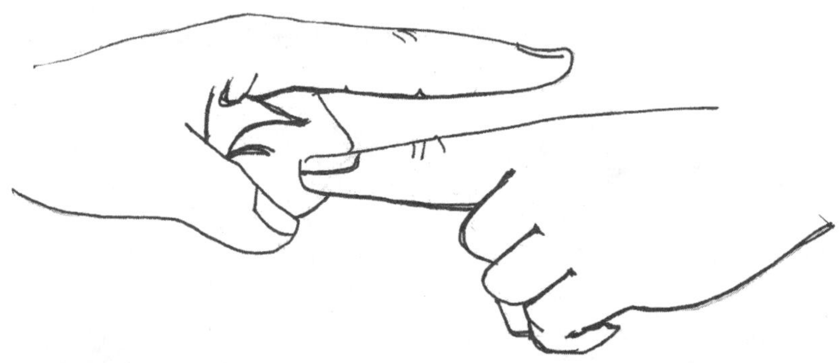

AGE 11+

SUBJECT: The Fall

BIBLE READING: Genesis 2:15–17; 3:1–13

DRAMA NOTES: This drama has one main speaking part (the narrator). The other characters speak one or two lines each. It could be used as part of an Easter service.

Cast: Narrator, Adam, Eve, Martin, Jake, Jake's parents (Adam and Eve may double), MP.
Staging: Drama opens with narrator centre stage, on his/her right is a baby doll in a manger, on his/her left are Adam and Eve.
Props: Doll in manger.

(while narrator is speaking Eve mimes picking fruit and offering it to Adam who takes and eats it)

Narrator: In the Garden of Eden, when time began
the friendship was close between God and man.
One fruit was forbidden. God told Adam why.
'If you eat fruit from that tree you will most surely die.'
But Adam ignored God. He ate from the tree,
which led to a mess of the highest degree.
The friendship was broken; death became fact.
All thanks to Adam and his sinful act.

Adam: Hey wait a minute! ***(points to Eve)*** What about Eve? Eating the fruit was ***her*** idea.

Narrator: As Adam points out, Eve ate the fruit first
so people might say her sin was the worst.

Eve: But they haven't heard the whole story. It was the snake. The snake tempted me.

Narrator: Adam passes the buck. Eve does the same.
Today their descendants still play the blame game.

(Adam and Eve exit – enter Martin & Co who stand in a row beside the narrator with their backs to the audience)

Narrator: Meet Martin. ***(turns Martin round)*** He hit an old man on the head;
made off with his wallet and left him for dead.

Martin: But listen – it wasn't my fault. I got in with a bad crowd. It was Jake. ***(turns Jake round)*** He made me do it.

Narrator: Jake's nasty and vicious. His mates live in fear.
It's thanks to this bully that Martin is here.

Jake: Yeah, well if I didn't look out for myself, no-one else would. My parents don't give a toss. ***(turns round parents)*** They're the ones you should be blaming.

Narrator: These are Jake's parents – Nancy and Pete.
They couldn't care less that Jake's on the street.

Nancy: Don't blame us for not caring!

Pete: You want to talk to this politician. ***(turns politician round)*** Ask how much caring ***she*** did?

Narrator: This is an MP who talked more and more,
while life became worse for the old and the poor.

MP: Now that's simply not fair. My party would have made life better for everyone if it hadn't been for the last government's mistakes. ***(moves as if he/she is going to fetch someone)***

Narrator: ***(stopping her)*** Sorry, we don't have room for anyone else.

(turns to audience) As you can see, the blame game goes on,
With a million excuses for all we do wrong.
And this is God's answer.

(lifts the baby from the manger)
A human. His Son,
who obeyed God in all things,
fought Satan and won.

(shows child to Martin who hangs head)
And we beat him up.

(shows child to Jake who hangs head)
We didn't care.

(shows child to Jake's parents who hang heads)
We made a cross.

(shows child to MP who hangs head)
And nailed him there.

(places doll back in cradle)
We'd no excuse.
We caused the pain.

(holds out arms as if on a cross)
But in his love
he took the blame.

Martin, Jake & Co: ***(look up, incredulously)*** He what!
(they turn towards the narrator who turns towards them arms outstretched as if to hug them)

Narrator: God took the blame for you and for me.
The blame game is over. His love sets us free.

APPLICATION

Theme: God's answer to sin

Explore: Adam and Eve

When Adam and Eve disobeyed God, it ruined their relationship with him. From then on every human being was infected by sin (Romans 5:12).

The snake

The snake or serpent who tempted Eve was Satan in disguise. Satan is the enemy of God – an angel who rebelled and was thrown out of heaven. God's words to the serpent in Genesis 3:15 (he will crush your head and you will strike his heel) point towards God's plan to defeat or crush Satan through his Son, Jesus Christ.

Chat

Act out some situations where people try and blame someone else e.g. when something gets damaged or when someone gets hurt. Chat about the reasons we blame others e.g. it can help us feel less guilty; it may mean we escape punishment. Chat about the benefits of owning up and saying sorry when we get things wrong.

Think

Thank God that he took the blame for us.

DRAMA 3

NO-BRAIN NOAH

AGE 8+

SUBJECT: Noah

BIBLE READING: Genesis 6:9–22

DRAMA NOTES: Suitable for reading in a group or for performance.

Cast: Narrator, Noah, Mrs Noah, Shem, Ham, Japeth, neighbours (2+).
Staging: Narrator far stage left. There should be a screen at the back onto which an image of an ark and then a rainbow can be projected.
Props: Overhead or data projector, screen, images of ark and rainbow, umbrellas, clipboard.

Narrator: Not long after God created the world, things went badly wrong. The people who lived on earth turned to evil. They spent their time hating and fighting and cared for no-one and nothing but themselves. ***(enter neighbours stage right, chanting and waving umbrellas as if they were swords)***

Neighbours: Two... four... six... eight... Attack, destroy and devastate. Two...four...six...eight... Attack, destroy and devastate.

Narrator: There was just one man – a farmer called Noah – who didn't join in their evil ways. Noah loved God and he taught his family to love God too. ***(enter Noah, Mrs Noah, Shem, Ham and Japeth chanting)***

Noah: Two... four... six... eight... Celebrate for God is great. Got that, everyone?

Shem & Co: Two... four... six... eight... Celebrate for God is great.

Narrator: One day God spoke to Noah. ***(Noah moves centre stage, adopts attitude of prayer)*** God said he was so tired of the evil people ***(neighbours mime fighting with umbrellas)*** he was going to send a flood – a flood so huge and so wet, it would wipe everyone out. Noah passed on God's message to his family. ***(Noah moves stage left)***

Noah: Listen, folks. I've something important to tell you – good news and bad news.

Mrs Noah: Tell us the bad news first.

Noah: All right. Here goes: there's going to be a terrible flood.

Mrs Noah: A flood! Oh no! It will ruin the carpets.

Noah: The good news is God has a plan to save us.

Mrs Noah: But not the carpets.

Noah: No dear, not the carpets.

Ham: So what ***is*** the plan?

Noah: God's plan for us is to survive by floating on top of the floodwaters. He's told me to build a huge boat with three decks, called an ark.

Mrs Noah: But… but… you're a farmer. You don't know anything about boat building.

Noah: Never mind that. This boat's a must… in God we trust… we'll build or bust. Got that, everyone?

Shem & Co: ***(exit chanting)*** This boat's a must… in God we trust…. we'll build or bust.

Narrator: So Noah built the ark. ***(sounds of hammering off stage)*** He made it exactly the way God said. And when it was finished, it looked amazing.

(ark is projected onto screen – enter Noah and family)

Shem: Wow, Dad, this boat is way bigger than our house!

Noah: That's because we need room for two of every kind of animal, insect and bird. God wants to save them too.

Narrator: Meanwhile Noah's neighbours kept making fun of him.

Neighbour 1: You've always been odd, Noah, But now you've ***really*** lost it. There isn't going to be a flood.

Noah: Oh yes there is.

Neighbour 1: Oh no there isn't.

Noah: Oh yes there is.

Neighbour 2: Oh no there isn't.

Noah: Oh yes there is. ***(exit Noah and family)***

Neighbours: ***(together, calling after them)*** Oh no there isn't.

Narrator: The neighbours made up a nasty chant about Noah.

Neighbours: ***(together)*** No mud, no rain… No flood, no brain… No-ah, No-ah. ***(repeat three times)***

Narrator: They kept this up right until the day Noah herded all the animals, birds and insects into the ark. Two by two the creatures went in through the door.

(enter Noah and family)

Noah: ***(consulting clipboard)*** Are the lions on board?

Shem: ***(points to ark)*** Yes – bottom deck.

Noah: And the monkeys?

Ham: ***(pointing)*** Yes – middle deck.

Noah: And the fleas?

Japeth: ***(scratching)*** I haven't seen them anywhere.

Mrs Noah: Don't worry, dear. The fleas are safe.

Noah: Great! That's it. On board everyone. ***(exit Noah and family)***

Narrator: Soon after that the whole sky darkened.

Neighbour 2: Oh dear! It looks as if we're in for a downpour. You don't think Noah could be right?

Neighbour 1: Right?! No-brain Noah! Of course not. ***(puts up umbrella)*** It's just a passing shower.

Narrator: But this wasn't a passing shower. ***(other neighbours put up umbrellas)*** This rain poured down steadily for forty days and forty nights until water covered the mountains and all life on earth was wiped out. ***(exit neighbours)***

Narrator: Inside the ark, though, everyone was safe.

(voices off-stage)

Noah: Have you mucked out the elephants yet, Ham?

Ham: Aw Dad, not the elephants! It's Shem's turn. I did them yesterday.

Narrator: Finally the rain stopped. The earth dried out and, at long last, Noah led the way out of the ark into a bright fresh world. ***(enter Noah and family)*** In the sky gleamed a beautiful rainbow. ***(rainbow is projected onto screen)***

Mrs Noah: Oh Noah! Smell the roses. This is wonderful!

Noah: ***(pointing at rainbow)*** Look dear, that rainbow is a sign of God's promise never to destroy the earth with a flood. The bad days are over. God wants us to work with him, caring for his world. Got that, everyone?

Shem & Co: Two… four… six… eight… with God we'll co-operate.

Noah: Four… six… eight… ten…

Shem & Co: He'll never flood the earth again.

Noah: Hip, hip…

Shem & Co: Hooray!

Noah: Hip, hip…

Shem & Co: Hooray!

Noah: Hip, hip…

Shem & Co: Hooray!

APPLICATION

Theme: Peer pressure

Explore: Noah

Ham's dad was a farmer called Noah. Noah's grandfather, Methuselah, holds the record for being the oldest person in the Bible. (He lived to be 969 – see Genesis 5:27.) In Hebrew, Noah's name means 'comfort'.

The Flood

In Matthew 24:38–9 Jesus tells his disciples that the end of the world will take people by surprise – just the way the flood did. God had a plan to save Noah and his family by keeping them safe in the Ark. Through Jesus, he has a plan to save people today.

Chat

Play a game where groups have a minute to look at a piece of coloured card with an irregularly shaped hole at the centre. They should then try and cut out their own shape to fit the hole. Bring out the card again and see who has produced the best match. Point out that in the world today, following Jesus will mean Christians sometimes feel that they don't fit in. Chat about why it is still best to live God's way.

Think

Ask children to think of a personal motto.

DRAMA 4

WE'RE MOVING

AGE 8+

SUBJECT: **God's call to Abram**

BIBLE READING: **Genesis 12:1–9**

DRAMA NOTES: To be performed by adults or young people.

Cast: Presenter, servant.

Presenter: Many years ago God spoke to a man called Abram. Now Abram wasn't young. He was a senior citizen – seventy-five, if he was a day. But God said to him, 'Abram, I want you to leave your country, your family and your relatives and go to the land that I will show you.' Wow! Imagine if your grandfather or great grandfather told you he'd got a message like that. It would be a bit of a shock wouldn't it?

Servant: ***(staggers in, wiping brow)*** Shock! Shock! I know all there is to know about shocks... ***(looks around)*** Wait a minute! Where am I? What century is this?

Presenter: It's the 21st century and you're in ________________. Here, have a seat. You look terrible.

Servant: ***(sits down)*** Thanks. ***(breathes deeply)*** That's better. My name is Eliezer. Can you get your tongue round that? El-i-ez-er. OK, you don't meet many Eliezers these days but I'm a 4000 year old Bible character and I've escaped from Old Testament times. I've come to your century because I really need a break. ***(sighs)*** You know how you feel when you've had a really rotten day at school... well I've just had THE WORST day at work.

Things began to go pear-shaped early this morning when I went to meet my master, Abram. I'm his head servant, you see. I went in, wearing my usual 'your-wish-is-my-command' sort of smile, expecting him to give me his usual 'you're-the-only-one-I-can-trust' sort of jobs: 'Eliezer, you're the only one I can trust to buy Sarai a bunch of figs for her birthday'; or 'Eliezer, you're the only one I can trust to road-test this camel.'

But today Abram was in an odd mood. Don't get me wrong. It wasn't a bad mood. Just ***odd.*** He didn't ask me to do anything. He seemed to be in another world, sitting staring into space. I had to clear my throat loudly three times before he even noticed I'd come in.

'Ah, there you are Eliezer,' says he (as if ***I'd*** kept ***him*** waiting!). Then he shakes his head, rubs his chin and calmly tells me a piece of news that makes my toes curl up in their sandals.

'Eliezer,' he says. 'We're moving to Canaan.'

'***Moving!***' I say.

'Yes, Eliezer. We need to pack up and get away as soon as possible.'

'To ***Canaan***,' I say.

'Yes, Eliezer. It's about a thousand miles from here.'

'***We***,' I say.

'Yes, Eliezer. Me and my family and my nephew Lot and his family and all our flocks and servants. And you're the only one I can trust to organise things.'

Arrghhh! At these words my head went fuzzy and my legs sort of wilted. Me – move a small army of people across miles of desert in an age when furniture vans haven't been invented! Somehow I managed to bow myself out of the room before I collapsed.

Of course, top class servant that I am, I soon pulled myself together. I've spent the rest of the day working flat out… gathering food, buying tents, loading camels. But the worst bit has been facing the neighbours… hearing folk say that Abram's mad and I should wise up and stay in Haran. Part of me would ***love*** to stay in Haran. But I won't. Because I know Abram ***isn't*** mad. He's a good man, is my master. He has a special relationship with God and he really believes this move is God's idea.

So, nothing else for it, I suppose. Better head back to my own century. You've a meeting to get on with and I've still a mountain of organising to do.

You know what, though – after talking to you, I'm beginning to get excited. I'm wondering what God has in store for us in Canaan. If I stayed put, I'd never know the answer. But I can't help feeling he's planning something BIG.

APPLICATION

Theme: God's plans

Explore: Abram

Abram grew up in a city called Ur. His father, Terah, set out to take the family to Canaan, but halfway there he decided they would settle in Haran. Abram, who was later called Abraham (Genesis 17:5) had a special covenant relationship with God. God promised him many descendants and he also promised to give him the land of Canaan (Genesis 17:3–8).

Chat

Has anyone in the group had to move to a new area? Chat about what it was like... the hard bits... the exciting bits. What was the story behind their move? Talk about the difference it can make to the way we feel about changes, if we know they are happening for a good reason.

Think

Ask the children to draw a life map showing some of the changes that have happened in their lives. Draw a big circle round the map to represent God's plan. Thank God that he knows everything about our lives, that he has BIG plans and we can be part of them.

DRAMA 5

A TWO-WAY PROMISE

AGE 6+

SUBJECT: **God's Covenant with Abraham**

BIBLE READING: **Genesis 15:1–21**

DRAMA NOTES: This drama has one main speaking part and eight small parts for children.

Cast: Abraham (should be played as an adult), 8 children.
Staging: Abraham centre stage. Children (each with a star) stand in a line behind Abraham with their backs to the audience.
Props: The letters C O V E N A N T printed on separate sheets of A4 paper and worn by the children. Eight silver stars on sticks. Mobile phone.

Abraham: Well, here I am in the 21st century. My name is Abraham, by the way, and I've some letters to show you. I'd love to tell you they were from people all saying I was their favourite Bible character. But the truth is these letters aren't fan mail. They're letters of the alphabet. And I want to use them to tell you a story. So the first letter I want you to meet is the letter **V.** ***(child 1 turns round and steps forward)***

Child 1: I am **V** for **Voice.**

Abraham: Not your voice or my voice. This **V** stands for ***God's* Voice.** And I've brought it along to remind us that at different times in my life God spoke to me. Sometimes he told ***me*** to do things and other times he told me things ***he*** was going to do. And that brings us to our next letter. ***(child 2 turns round and steps forward)***

Child 2: I am **E** for **Expect.**

Abraham: For many years there was one thing that was a big disappointment to me and my wife. We didn't have any children. I thought when I died it would be the end of my family. But one day, God spoke to me and told me to **Expect** miracles. He took me outside, got me to look up at the star-studded sky and gave me a promise. ***(child 3 turns round and steps forward)***

Child 3: I am **N** for **Number.**

Abraham: Yes, I know promise begins with the letter **P** but this **N** is here because God promised me I would have so many descendants I wouldn't be able to **Number** them any more than I could count the number of stars in the sky. But that wasn't all. He gave me a second promise about the land he'd led me to. ***(child 4 turns round and steps forward)***

Child 4: I am **C** for **Canaan.**

Abraham: Back then the land of Canaan belonged to the Kenites, Kenizzites, Kadmonites, Hittites and loads of other tribes I just call 'parasites' for short. Anyway, that day God promised the whole land would one day belong to my family. And the next letter stands for the way I felt. ***(child 5 turns round and steps forward)***

Child 5: I am **A** for **Ah.**

Abraham: I don't know what sort of sound you make when you gasp… but I sort of go 'Ahhh'. I was **Ah-bsolutely Ah-mazed.** I believed God, but I just wanted to double check I'd got it right. So I asked him to tell me how I could be really sure this would happen. ***(child 6 turns round and steps forward)***

Child 6: I am **O** for **Offering.**

Abraham: God told me to make him an **Offering.** I was to sacrifice a cow, a goat, a sheep, a dove and a pigeon to show my faith. It was almost dark by the time I got everything ready, so can I have my **N** back? **N** for **Night.** ***(beckons over to child 3)***

Child 3: I am **N** for **Number.**

Abraham: No, this time I want you to be **N** for **Night.** ***(child shakes head)*** Oh, you've a problem with that, have you? ***(child nods)*** So what am I meant to do?

Child 3: You could phone a friend…

Abraham: If you insist. ***(takes out mobile)*** Hello, I'd like to order a letter N. What's that? No, no sauce, thanks. ***(child 7 turns round and steps forward)*** Great! Thank you.

Child 7: I am **N** for **Night.**

Abraham: And you are also **N** for **NEVER,** because I could **NEVER** forget what happened that **NIGHT.** I fell into a deep sleep and as I slept God showed me the future. He told me my descendants would spend 400 years as slaves in another land before being brought back to Canaan. I woke up then and saw something incredible – a smoking pot and a blazing torch moving between the pieces of meat I was sacrificing. I knew I was right in the presence of the living God, and that these promises were for real. ***(as Abraham speaks he should be rearranging children into the first 7 letters of the word covenant)*** So let's have a look at the letters we've got so far. They make up the first seven letters of a really important Bible word – a word to do with promises. All we need to finish is a **T.** ***(child 8 turns round and runs to end of line)*** And here she/he is.

Child 8: I am **T** for **Two.**

Abraham: Excellent. We've got the word **C O V E N A N T** and our **T** here stands for **Two** because a **Covenant** is a special kind of two-way promise. God promises to do His part and we promise to do ours. My part, back then, was simply to believe what God said… and these stars ***(children hold up stars)*** …these stars represent all the descendants God gave me. He kept his word to me, just in the same way as he'll keep his word to you. So remember a covenant is a two-way promise. And let's give our stars a big round of applause… ***(children bow)***

APPLICATION

Theme: God's promises

Explore: God's Covenant with Abraham

A covenant is a special kind of promise. When God made his covenant with Abram he gave him and his wife Sarai the new names of Abraham and Sarah (Genesis 17:5,15). The name Abraham means 'father of a multitude of nations'.

Chat

Look up some of the promises that God has made to us today through Jesus. Promises about eternal life (John 6:51), about being with us (Matthew 28:20), about our relationship with him (John 15:14), about prayer (John 14:12–14). Chat about our side of these promises – the things we need to do to see them working out in our lives.

Think

Children could copy one of God's promises onto a blank postcard. They can write their names on the back of the card. Suggest they use this as a reminder that these weren't just promises Jesus made to his followers 2000 years ago. They are promises he makes to us today.

DRAMA 6

WHAT A LAUGH!

AGE 8+

SUBJECT: **The Birth of Isaac**

BIBLE READING: **Genesis 21:1–7**

DRAMA NOTES: This monologue is best performed by an adult or young person in costume. Children should be encouraged to respond at the points marked *.

Cast: Sarah.
Props: Words 'LAUGH' 'LAF' 'LAFTER' and 'AFTER' printed out to be shown at appropriate times.

Sarah: My name is Sarah and I want to talk to you about laughing. First let's just check if you know how to spell the word 'laugh'. That's right – LAUGH*. Really to make life simpler I think the word should be spelt LAF which means laughter would be spelt LAFTER which makes a whole lot more sense, especially when you remember you usually laugh AFTER something happens. I mean, people mostly laugh for a reason. If you saw someone going round laughing at nothing... well, you'd wonder about them, wouldn't you?

I can honestly say I laughed a lot in my earthly life. I lived to be 127 and I laughed most days at least once. Often it was because I found something funny. Maybe my husband Abraham cracked a corny joke, or I was milking a goat and squirted myself. But sometimes I laughed because I was embarrassed or even because I wanted a couple of servants, who were trying it on, to know that I didn't believe a word they said. The fact is, we laugh for lots of different reasons and those reasons affect the sort of sound we make. Just to prove that... let's do a little experiment. Let's see if we can make some different-sounding laughs...

Can you give me a nervous laugh?*

Or an unkind laugh?*

Or a loud, silly laugh?*

You know, looking back, I remember a day when I laughed and afterwards I felt really bad about it.

I was ninety years old at the time and I laughed that day because I'd just overheard an angel tell my husband Abraham that inside a year I'd have a baby. Could you credit it? There was this angelic messenger giving my husband the most brilliant news ever – that we were about to have the child we'd hoped and waited and prayed for right through our married life – and all I could do was laugh. What's more it was the wrong sort of laugh – a doubting, 'as if' sort of laugh.

'I'm an old woman,' I thought. 'Ninety year old women don't have babies.' And so I laughed.

But of course that was reckoning without God. I believed in God. And almost immediately I was sorry for my unbelieving laugh. I'm sorry still, especially as it's there in the Bible for everyone to read about.

The good thing is, though, that folk can also read about me laughing in a very different way... twelve months later... when my baby arrived. That was the best laugh of my life. I was just bursting with joy and thankfulness. There I was – ninety-one years of age – holding my own baby in my arms. God had kept his promise. He'd given Abraham and me a son. He'd even given us the child's name. 'Call him Isaac,' God told us... and can you guess what that means?* The name Isaac means 'he laughs'.

APPLICATION

Theme: Laughter

Explore: Sarah

Sarai married Abram, who was actually her half brother (see Genesis 20:12), when they were living in Ur. She later moved with him to Canaan. Shortly before Isaac was born God changed her name to Sarah and promised that she would be the mother of nations (Genesis 17:15,16).

Chat

Show ten minutes of a funny video e.g. an episode of Mr Bean. Chat about the difference between someone laughing at Mr Bean and someone laughing at someone who falls over in the street or at the speaker in a youth group 'God slot'.

Think

The birth of a baby brings a lot of joy, but also lots of responsibilities. Pray with the children for families they know where there is a new baby.

BLIND DATE

AGE 10+

SUBJECT: **Isaac and Rebekah**

BIBLE READING: **Genesis 24:62–66**

DRAMA NOTES: Suitable for reading in a group or for performance. Non-narrative parts could be acted by puppets.

Cast: Two narrators, servant, camel, Rebekah, Abraham.
Staging: Narrators together left of a large screen, above which the upper bodies of the servant and camel are visible.

Narrator 1: We're here to tell you a love story.

Narrator 2: A story about this servant and his camel.

Camel: ***(moving amorously towards servant)*** A ***love*** story! Fancy that! I didn't know you cared!

Servant: ***(pushing camel away)*** I don't. Get off!

Narrator 2: The servant has been sent to find a bride for his master's son. He has been on the road for days and now he has reached a spring.

Camel: ***(jumping)*** Spring... spring... spring...

Servant: It's a watering-hole type spring, you silly beast.

Camel: You mean I can stop jumping. That's a relief! So why are we here?

Servant: We're here because our master, Abraham, wants Isaac to marry a girl from his own clan.

Camel: And Abraham's clan lives near this spring – right?

Servant: ***(hesitating)*** Well... Abraham's directions weren't clear. It's over a hundred years since he left these parts.

Narrator 1: Hold on a minute. Are we saying this servant is expected to track down a girl who's related to Isaac – who just happens to be the sort of girl Isaac can fall for – who just happens to be ready to leave everything she's ever known to marry a man she's never met? And he isn't even sure if he's come to the right place?

Narrator 2: ***(nodding)*** Yep.

(while they're speaking servant sinks his head into his hands and looks more and more depressed)

Camel: ***(brightly)*** There's nothing we like more than a challenge... a really ***impossible*** challenge.

Narrator 1: If you ask me there's as much chance of that servant finding Miss Right as of his camel being bridesmaid at the wedding.

Camel: I could do it, I could do it!

Narrator 2: Aren't you forgetting something?

Narrator 1: I don't think so.

Narrator 2: Abraham prayed for an angel to guide his servant.

Narrator 1: So where is this angel? Didn't it get the message? ***(leans towards microphone)*** This is a staff announcement. Would the angel supposed to be guiding Abraham's servant please report to the spring.

Narrator 2: The angel is invisible. But its presence gives the servant faith.

Servant: ***(looks up)*** Surely God has brought us to this very spring, at this very time, on this very day.

Camel: ***(nodding vigorously)*** We're here… because we're here… because we're here… because…

Servant: ***(interrupting)*** So I'm going to ask God for a sign. ***(drops to knees)*** Dear God, when the next girl comes to get water I'll say to her, 'Please, give me a drink'. If she's the right girl, please make her offer to fetch a drink for my camel too.

Narrator 2: No sooner has the servant finished praying than a girl appears.

(Rebekah appears above screen)

Narrator 1: Hey, are you sure that isn't the angel. She looks like an angel to me.

Narrator 2: She's a ***girl*** and her name is Rebekah.

Servant: ***(approaches Rebekah)*** Please give me a little water from your jug.

Rebekah: Of course.

(camel pants loudly)

Rebekah: Your camel sounds thirsty.

(camel pants more loudly than ever)

Rebekah: I'll fetch some water for him too. ***(she disappears below screen)***

Camel: ***(leaping up and down in excitement)*** It's the sign... the sign.

(Rebekah reappears and gives water to camel)

Servant: Er... I suppose you wouldn't happen to be related to an Abraham, son of Terah, who used to live around here?

Rebekah: Abraham is my great uncle.

Narrator 1: Hurrah! The servant has found a relative. She's the one!

Servant: Hallelujah!

Narrator 1: And so, praising God for guiding him, the servant sweeps Rebekah onto his camel and gallops straight back to Canaan.

Servant, Camel and Rebekah: What!?

Narrator 2: Ignore that! What really happens is that the servant goes home with Rebekah to meet her family, explain what he wants and give everyone time to make up their minds.

(servant, camel and Rebekah disappear below screen)

Narrator 1: But... but... that's ***risky***. What if Rebekah or her parents say 'no'?

Narrator 2: The good news is they say 'yes'. The servant gets the go-ahead and Rebekah sets off with him for Canaan.

Narrator 1: Whew...

(servant, camel and Rebekah reappear and move along screen)

Narrator 2: As the group draw near to Abraham's place, Rebekah spots a man out in a field. The man spots Rebekah. Their eyes meet. It's love at first sight. She runs off to meet him.

(Rebekah points, clasps hand to chest, then disappears)

Narrator 1: Oh dear!

Narrator 2: What do you mean, 'Oh dear!'

Narrator 1: She's meant to fall in love with Isaac.

Narrator 2: The man ***is*** Isaac, you bonehead.

(old man appears – he goes over to servant and camel)

Abraham: This is wonderful. Rebekah is perfect... perfect in every way.

Narrator 1: Are you telling me Rebekah has fallen in love with ***him?***

Narrator 2: Give me patience. That isn't Isaac. That's Abraham – he's come to thank his faithful servant for all that he's done

Abraham: Thank you, my dear servant, thank you.

Camel: No probs! It was easy peasy. And now I'm going to be bridesmaid. Right?

Servant: Wrong! ***(pushes camel below screen. He and Abraham exit together)***

Narrator 1: Well, the camel may not be bridesmaid, but I've learnt something from that story.

Narrator 2: You have? No, don't tell me. You're going to say something silly...

Narrator 1: I was just going to say you can't get servants like that these days…

Narrator 2: I knew it.

Narrator 1: No… wait… I haven't finished. You can't get servants but you can get guidance. Our God is a God who still hears and answers prayer.

APPLICATION

Theme: Guidance

Explore: Isaac and Rebekah

Isaac was forty years old when he married Rebekah (Genesis 25:20). Before she came into his life he had been feeling sad because his mother had died (Genesis 23:1–2). Rebekah comforted him (Genesis 24:67). Twenty years later Isaac and Rebekah had twin boys, Jacob and Esau (Genesis 25:25,26).

Chat

Open a box of chocolates. Before passing it round talk about how the children will decide which one to pick. The manufacturers know people often need help in choosing, which is why they include a little leaflet showing each chocolate and saying what's inside. Choosing a chocolate is a small decision. Chat about the bigger decisions – about where and how we can get help. When we pray about decisions, God does not always answer instantly and dramatically – but the Bible can be a little bit like the leaflet in the box of chocolates giving us the information we need to make the right choice.

Think

Think about the words of Psalm 32:8, 'I will instruct you and teach you in the way you should go. I will counsel you and watch over you.' Thank God that this is his promise to us.

DRAMA 8

QUICK FIX

AGE 10+

SUBJECT: **Esau's Birthright**

BIBLE READING: **Genesis 25:27–34**

DRAMA NOTES: This is a monologue for reading or performance by a leader. Beforehand another leader should explain what a birthright is (see Explore section).

Cast: Esau.

Esau: Well, this is a surprise! One minute I'm just home from a hunting trip and the next I'm here in your meeting. And you know what – I didn't have time to wash before leaving. So I'm sweaty, ***(wipes brow)*** and I'm smelly. ***(sniffs under armpits)*** But I'll tell you one good thing. I'm not hungry… which means you don't have to feed me… ***(pats tummy)*** I'm stuffed full of red lentil stew. Mmmm. ***(runs tongue round lips)*** I can still taste it. In fact I think there are a couple of lentils still stuck in my teeth. ***(pokes finger in mouth and chews)***

Yeah! That stew my brother made was magic. My name's Esau by the way. I'm the hunter in our family and my brother Jacob is the cook. Give Jake a jar of oil and a handful of flour and he'll turn out pastry that would melt in your mouth. He's a dead loss with a bow and arrow, though. Good at making buns but no good at shooting them. Ha! Ha! Buns… Bunnies… Get it?

Anyway, this evening I got back from my bunny-hunting trip only to find Jake in the kitchen stirring this steaming pot of lentil stew. And it suddenly hit me – I was famished. Not just a little bit famished, but famished like it felt my stomach had turned into this gaping quarry and my rib cage was about to cave in.

'Quick! I need food,' I gasped.

'Hands off!' Jake steps between me and the stove and throws me a scheming look. 'I want something in exchange,' says he. 'I want you to give me your birthright.'

Well, at this my chin sort of hit my chest. I mean if he'd asked me for two weeks' pocket money, or a couple of pheasants, or my favourite sheepskin slippers, I'd have understood it. But my birthright? Something you can't spend, or eat, or wear. I mean you can't do anything with a birthright… it's just a sort of a promise for the future… about inheriting stuff… something that comes with being an eldest son.

It took me all of two seconds to make up my mind. At that moment I'd have done anything… sung a solo, shaved my head, sold my granny… anything for a decent meal. And all Jacob wanted was a stupid birthright.

'Fine. It's yours,' I shrugged.

'Swear that it's mine!' says Jacob.

So I swore that it was. 'I promise you my birthright. OK. Now give me some food.'

Mmmmm. Like I said, that stew tasted good.

Only trouble is it was over so fast. Six gulps and a gobble and it was gone. And now... well, I'm about to put the whole business right out of my head. OK, so maybe selling my birthright for a plate of stew wasn't the smartest thing to do... but hey, who cares! I'm not going to think about the future or about what will happen when Dad pops his clogs. When I'm bored, I shoot things. When I'm hungry, I eat. For me the important thing is living for the moment. I want to have everything I want right now.

APPLICATION

Theme: Temptation

Explore: Birthrights

In Old Testament times the first born son ranked highest in the family after the father. He would also inherit twice as much (a double portion) as any other son after his father died and would become the leader of the family. An eldest son could sell or give away his birthright but, if he did that, he gave up his rights to the blessings that were his by birth.

Esau

Esau was Isaac and Rebekah's eldest son – but only by a few minutes. Esau had a twin brother Jacob, who was born holding onto Esau's heel (Genesis 25:26). Esau gave away his birthright without a thought, but later he had a lot of regrets. In Hebrews 12:14–17 the story of Esau selling his birthright is held up as a warning. Don't swap the spiritual blessing of eternal life for a 'living for the moment' quick fix.

Chat

Talk about tempting situations. Ask children to act out a situation where someone is tempted to do something they know is wrong just to get some instant satisfaction. Chat about the best ways to beat temptation (praying, avoiding the situation, practising saying 'no').

Think

Consider the words in the Lord's prayer, 'Lead us not into temptation'. Thank God that he is always ready to answer that prayer.

DRAMA 9

AN UGLY STORY

AGE 10+

SUBJECT: **Jacob and Esau (Jacob's deceit)**

BIBLE READING: **Genesis 27:1–13**

DRAMA NOTES:

Cast: Two narrators, 2 + helpers to hold objects above screen.
Staging: Narrators stand on either side of a screen above which objects are held as indicated by an * and the numbers below.
Props: (1) Card with the words *Lies, deceit, betrayal.* (2) Cuddly toy. (3) Hairy wig. (4) Hair gel. (5) Mail order catalogue. (6) Wooden spoon. (7) Football. (8) Mohair pullover or cardigan. (9) Card with the words *New life, forgiveness.*

Narrator 1: This is an ugly story. It's a story full of lies, deceit, betrayal*(1) and the death of furry creatures*(2).

Narrator 2: It is also a story full of hair*(3).

Narrator 1: The hair*(3) belonged to a guy called Esau. Esau was a muscular, out-of-doors sort of chap who could have survived in a jungle no problem. He'd have been perfect for 'I'm a celebrity get me out of here' – except he wasn't a celebrity. He wasn't talented or glamorous. He wasn't even very bright. On second thoughts maybe he was celebrity material after all!

Narrator 2: Anyway hairy Esau*(3) had a well-groomed twin brother, Jacob*(4). They were twins but Esau had been born first. Jacob was a real smoothie. He'd have made a brilliant salesman*(5). He had brains, and wheeling and dealing came as naturally to him as sleep.

Narrator 1: Now to make sense of this story you need to understand that, in Old Testament times, getting your father's blessing meant a lot. It set you up to become head of the family when the old head died. You were like the head's hair*(3) – heir… Get it?! And of course, being the eldest twin, hairy Esau expected to become his father Isaac's heir.

Narrator 2: So it happened that one day, old Isaac, who'd lost his sight, but not his appetite, called Esau to his side.

Narrator 1: 'Go hunting, my son'…

Narrator 2: …he said.

Narrator 1: 'And then prepare me a tasty meal with what you catch and I will give you my blessing before I die.'

Narrator 2: Esau grabbed his bow.

Narrator 1: 'Righty ho, Dad'…

Narrator 2: …he said. And off he went.

Narrator 1:.Which is where the lies, deceit, betrayal*(1) and death of furry creatures*(2) come in.

Narrator 2: Earywigging on this conversation was 'The Mummy'*(6).

Narrator 1: You haven't met 'The Mummy'*(6) yet. Her name was Rebekah and she was the sort of mother who watches football*(7) matches from the side-lines and has eyes for only one player...

Narrator 2: ...her son.

Narrator 1: And in Isaac's household, Mummy Rebekah had eyes for only one son and that was Jacob*(4). She'd made up her mind that he, not Esau, should become her blind husband's heir.

Narrator 2: 'Jacob, your father's about to give his blessing to Esau. I want you to go outside and kill a couple of goats*(2)'...

Narrator 1: ...she said.

Narrator 2: 'I'll*(6) make a tasty meal for you to take to your Dad, so instead of giving the blessing to Esau, he'll give it to you.'

Narrator 1: The Bible doesn't tell us what Jacob was doing at the time, but it is not hard to imagine him wondering how on earth he'll kill two goats without creasing his robe and getting his hands dirty. And of course, with his salesman's*(5) brain, Jacob instantly spots the one thing that could stop Isaac buying this.

Narrator 2: Hair*(3) – or rather, not enough of it. He said...

Narrator 1: ...'Esau is hairy and I'm not. What if Dad feels me?'

Narrator 2: But the Mummy*(6) had this sorted. She said...

Narrator 1: ...'Don't worry. We'll wrap your arms in goatskin*(8). That way he'll never know the difference.'

Narrator 2: And so it all came about just as we warned – the lies, the deceit, the betrayal*(1) and the death of furry creatures*(2).

Narrator 1: Jacob killed the goats.

Narrator 2: Rebekah made the stew.

Narrator 1: Jacob took the stew to Isaac.

Narrator 2: Isaac felt the hair on his arms*(8), gave him his blessing and, by the time poor old Esau came home from hunting, everything was done and dusted.

Narrator 1: He'd lost his inheritance. His brother was set to be the new family head.

Narrator 2: Now maybe you're wondering how such an ugly story got into the Bible?

Narrator 1: Why would God want anyone reading stuff like that?

Narrator 2: Well, one thing we need to remember is that the story doesn't end there.

Narrator 1: Jacob's actions had consequences.

Narrator 2: One being that he had to leave home to stop Esau placing his big hairy hands around his neck and breaking it.

Narrator 1: But the story doesn't end there either. No, in the end the story of Jacob and Esau shows that the world is divided.

Narrator 2: It is divided into people who have hair*(3)...

Narrator 1: ...and people who haven't.

Narrator 2: But more importantly, into people who look for forgiveness...

Narrator 1: ...and people who don't.

Narrator 2: And the great thing is that Jacob ended up in the first group.

Narrator 1: He didn't get any hairier*(3) but he did realise he'd gone badly wrong and that he needed to put things right.

Narrator 2: Far away from home he put things right with God and then he risked everything to put things right with his brother.

Narrator 1: So I suppose you could say this is a story where, in the end, God brought forgiveness and new life*(9)...

Narrator 2: ...which means it's not such an ugly story after all.

APPLICATION

Theme: Repentance

Explore: Jacob

Jacob is a very important Old Testament character. His name was later changed to Israel. He had twelve sons and their descendants became the twelve tribes of Israel – God's chosen people. His story shows that God doesn't write people off just because they get off to a bad start. After his lies and deceit, Jacob had to leave home and stay with his mother's brother, Laban, in Haran. God met with him as he travelled and Jacob's character began to change as a result.

Chat

We don't have to look very hard to find examples of 'ugly' stories. Talk about one or two you may have heard about on the news or read in the newspapers. Ugly stories stay ugly when people refuse to change their ways or learn from their mistakes. Then see if you can think of an ugly story where God brought new life, e.g. the story of 'Catchem' the Highwayman in *Fifty stories for Special Occasions* (Children's Ministry).

Think

Has anyone ever played a mean trick on you? Ask God to help you forgive them. Have you done something sneaky or mean to somebody else? Ask God to help you put things right.

DRAMA 10

RACHEL'S WEDDING

AGE 11+

SUBJECT: **Rachel and Leah**

BIBLE READING: **Genesis 29:14–30**

DRAMA NOTES: This may be performed as a straight monologue or as a monologue with mime to music.

Cast: Rachel or Narrator *(Rachel's Voice)*, Rachel, Leah, Laban, Jacob.
Staging: Mime – scene opens with Rachel centre stage. Narrator is hidden from view.
Props: Wigs, face paint (especially for Rachel and Leah), music, CD player.

Narrator: Yesterday ought to have been the happiest day of my life. At long last I was to marry my cousin Jacob. ***(Jacob enters and stands beside Rachel)***

I fell for him the moment he showed up on our farm. ***(they turn to each other)*** The local boys could hardly string two words together but he was fun. He told me stories, jokes and family stuff about how he'd run away from home because his brother wanted him dead. ***(Jacob mimes strangling)***

And then, after a few weeks, he talked about us. ***(Jacob takes Rachel's hand)*** He wanted to marry me ***(Jacob kisses her hand)***, but Father expected flocks and money for my hand ***(Laban enters and snatches Rachel)*** and Jacob had nothing… no flocks, no silver, no gold, no land. ***(Jacob shows empty pockets)*** So he offered to spend seven years working on the farm for free. ***(Jacob pleading gesture)***

Father let everyone think he was doing us a favour. He kept stroking my hair and saying he'd rather give his beautiful daughter to a relative than a neighbour. ***(Laban puts arm round Rachel)***

Notice he said his ***beautiful*** daughter. Leah – my elder sister – isn't beautiful. ***(Leah enters)*** I'm the one whose hair is thick and dark, whose lips are red. Leah's so plain. If her eyes weren't weak, she'd want a bag for her head. ***(Laban looks at Leah and shakes his head. He leads her offstage)***

So Jacob spent seven whole years working for Father without pay. Sometimes I'd pout and grumble, then he'd kiss me and say, ***(Jacob puts his arm round Rachel)*** 'Dreaming of my beautiful Rachel makes time fly.' And yesterday, at long last it came – our big day. ***(Laban leads Leah back on stage. Leah has her face covered by a veil. Rachel steps back. Jacob turns to greet his bride)***

To the guests it looked like any other wedding. Fancy food, fine wine, a trembling bride, her father slapping the bridegroom on the shoulder, making him drink more and more. ***(Laban gives Leah to Jacob)*** But the truth is, the wedding was a sham. ***(Jacob puts his arm round Leah)*** The bride behind the thick veil wasn't me. I was shrieking for help, tied up on a cave floor ***(Rachel comes forward, mimes struggling to free herself from ropes)*** while squinting Leah stole my place. And Jacob didn't know until, too late, he saw her face. ***(Jacob lifts veil – Jacob turns away in shock and steps back. Leah runs to Laban – they step back)***

How ***could*** they! My father! Leah! ***(Rachel points back at them. Leah hangs head)*** Of course she says she had no choice. She's the elder sister. Father made her marry first.

But why should I have to suffer because Leah's on the shelf? ***(Rachel buries head in hands)*** Between them, they ruined ***everything.***

(Jacob comes to her) Except, of course, as Jacob says, they can't rob us of our love.

'We've got to trust God, Rachel,' he said, kissing away my tears. ***(Jacob pulls her hands from her face)*** 'Your father's promised I can marry you next week, if I work for seven more years.' ***(Leah steps forward. Jacob takes her hand so that he is standing with her on one side and Rachel on the other)***

Well I suppose next week is better than never. That doesn't make it all right, though. ***(Rachel steps out in front of Leah and Jacob, looks up, palms upward, as if speaking to God)*** I'm Jacob's first love. Why should I be his second wife? God help me let this disappointment go.

APPLICATION

Theme: Disappointment

Explore: Rachel and Leah

In Old Testament times it was common practice for a man to have more than one wife. Leah, Jacob's first wife, had six sons and one daughter. (Reuben, Simeon, Levi, Judah, Issachar, Zebulun and Dinah) For many years Rachel had no children, then she had a son, Joseph, and later died giving birth to her second son, Benjamin. Jacob had four other sons, Dan, Naphtali, Gad and Asher. (Genesis 29:31—30:22 and 35:16–18).

Chat

Talk about the sort of things that make us feel disappointed. Then ask the group to imagine they've got the job of writing a letter to Rachel to help her get over her disappointment. What would they say?

Think

Share a time when you have been disappointed. Explain how God helped you get over it.

DRAMA 11

THREE BLIND VULTURES

AGE 8+

SUBJECT: **Jacob and Esau are reconciled**

BIBLE READING: **Genesis 33:1–10** (to be read after drama)

DRAMA NOTES: The audience is involved throughout the drama in creating sound effects that should be written out on cue cards and orchestrated by the narrator. *If the vultures are self-conscious about singing, the words in brackets […] may be omitted.*

Cast: Narrator, three vultures (wearing dark glasses), an owl (wearing large spectacles).

Staging: Narrator stage right, three vultures centre stage, owl stage left.

Props: Three pairs of dark glasses, large spectacles, cue cards as follows – 'stamp feet x 4', 'teeth chattering x 4', 'baa x 3', 'hiss x 3', 'moo x 3', 'hee-haw x 3', 'fast stamp x 8', 'kisses x 4', 'boo-hoo x 4', 'hurrah x 1', 'clapping and cheering'.

Narrator: On a cliff overlooking a plain in the land of Canaan lived three blind birds. ***(birds squawk)*** The three birds were vultures. Their names were Wary Vulture, Hairy Vulture and Scary Vulture [and they had their own song. It went like this:

Vultures:
(to tune of three blind mice)

Three blind birds, three blind birds.
See how we flap, see how we flap.
We fly overhead as the battles begin.
When they are over, that's when we swoop in
We land on the bodies and peck at their skin.
We're three blind birds.]

Narrator: A wise owl also lived on the cliff. ***(owl hoots)*** [This wise owl didn't have a song, which, now that you've heard from the vultures, just goes to show how wise it was.]

Now the three vultures might not have been able to see much, but there was nothing wrong with their hearing. Their ears were sharp enough to pick up the faintest movement on the plain. They spent their time listening and the wise owl helped them understand what was going on.

One day the birds heard the sound of an army. ***(stamp feet on ground x 4)***

Vultures: What do those marching feet mean?

Owl: Those feet belong to 400 armed men. Esau, the son of Isaac, is leading them out to meet his brother Jacob.

Narrator: The blind birds listened again and this time they heard the sound of chattering teeth. ***(teeth chattering x 4)***

Vultures: What do those chattering teeth mean?

Owl: Those teeth belong to Jacob and the women and children with him. Their teeth are chattering because they fear for their lives.

Narrator: Then the owl explained that years earlier Esau and Jacob had fallen out.

Owl: Jacob stole Esau's blessing and Esau vowed to kill him. So Jacob ran away. He's stayed away for years and years. But now he's coming home.

Narrator: This news made the blind birds squawk with delight.

Wary: Oh sweet one! This is Esau's chance to get his own back.

Hairy: There'll be a huge battle.

Scary: With lots of bodies for us to feed on.

Narrator: The wise owl did not answer. Sadly it flew to the other side of the cliff, ***(exit owl)*** leaving the birds eagerly waiting for the kill. But instead of the sounds of death, they heard something else. First came the sound of goats maa-ing. ***(maa x 3)***

Vultures: Very strange.

Narrator: Then sheep baa-ing. ***(baa x 3)***

Vultures: Seriously weird.

Narrator: Then camels spitting. ***(hiss x 3)***

Vultures: How rude!

Narrator: Then cows mooing ***(moo x 3)*** and donkeys braying. ***(hee-haw x 3)***

Vultures: We're confused.

Narrator: Finally, as the sun went down, the blind birds heard a man praying. The man prayed all night long, and in the morning new sounds came thick and fast.

Wary: I hear the sound of running steps. ***(stamp feet on ground fast x 8)***

Hairy: I hear the sound of kissing lips. ***(kisses x 4)***

Scary: I hear the sound of human tears. ***(boo-hoo x 4)***

Wary: I hear the sound of children's cheers. ***(hurrah x 1)***

Narrator: Next thing, the wise owl returned with a triumphant hoot. ***(enter owl)***

Owl: Twit… twit… twoorrah! There isn't going to be a battle. Esau has kissed his brother. He's accepted a huge maa-ing, baa-ing, spitting, mooing, braying present of animals. Jacob's prayers have been answered. The brothers are friends!

Narrator: When the birds heard this they were disgusted.

Wary: But… but… we're ***starving.***

Hairy: It isn't ***fair***.

Scary: We wanted them to ***kill*** each other.

Narrator: The wise owl looked the blind birds up and down.

Owl: What are you like?

Narrator: Pathetic. Losers. Heartless. Those are the words that spring to mind… ***(vultures droop)*** …but that wasn't what the wise owl saw.

Owl: I see that you don't ***have*** to be like this. You could change.

Vultures: Change! Us! But how?

Owl: Wary, give me a 'doh'.

Wary: ***(singing)*** Doh.

Owl: Hairy, give me a 'ray'.

Hairy: ***(singing)*** Ray.

Owl: Scary, give me a 'me'.

Scary: ***(singing)*** Me.

Owl: Yes, I thought so. You've got the sound. You've got the look. As a BIRD BAND you could be the next BIG THING.

Narrator: So let's hear it for ***The Vultures,*** folks. Come on, give them a big hand.

(clapping and cheering)

APPLICATION

Theme: Meetings

Explore: Jacob's meetings with God

Many years after Jacob ran away from his brother Esau, God told him to go back home. Jacob knew he needed to put things right with Esau but it was a big risk. The night before he met with his brother, Jacob wrestled for hours with a mysterious stranger, who represented God. At daybreak, the stranger blessed Jacob (Genesis 32:22-27). After Jacob met with Esau, God met with Jacob again (Genesis 35:9-13). God told him that from now on his name would be Israel (meaning 'he struggles with God') and promised to give him the land of Canaan.

Chat

Chat about times when the children have felt nervous or worried about meeting someone (maybe after a quarrel). What did they do beforehand? How did it go? Discuss how God can help us put things right when we fall out with friends or family.

Think

Jacob gave the name 'Bethel' (meaning House of God) to the place where he wrestled with God. God can meet with us anywhere, but sometimes it helps to have a special place or places where we go to pray. Ask the children to think of places which are special to them.

DRAMA 12

DREAM ON

AGE 7+

SUBJECT: Joseph's Dreams

BIBLE READING: Genesis 37:1–11

DRAMA NOTES: This is an interactive drama. Beforehand the group should be told to shake hands with a partner every time they hear the word **brothers**. When they hear the word **bow** or **bowed**, they bow. It may be performed as a monologue with Joseph as the only speaker or parts for Joseph's brothers, mother and father may be included as indicated below.

Cast: Joseph *or* Joseph, 3+ brothers, mother, father.
Staging: (for version 2) Joseph stage left – brothers, mother and father in a group stage right.
Props: Cardboard illustrations of sun, moon and stars attached to sticks.

Joseph: I had eleven **brothers.** ***(brothers wave)*** My parents called me Joe.
I lived with them in Canaan, many years ago.
Our house was never empty. Still I felt alone.
My **brothers** seemed to hate me. ***(brothers shake fists)*** When I spoke, they'd groan.
The trouble was that Father ***(father waves)*** had always loved me best,
And showed it with a gift that made me stand out from the rest.
It was a many-coloured coat. With fine thread it was sewed.
But every time I wore it, my **brothers** called me

Brothers: 'Toad!'

Joseph: Then one night I dreamt that I was working on our farm,
Working with my **brothers**, bringing sheaves into our barn. ***(brothers mime working)***
And suddenly the sheaf, which I was binding up with twine,
Rose upright, while my **brothers'** sheaves all **bowed** down to mine.
I found this dream so startling I sat up straight in bed
And shared it with my **brothers.**

Brothers: 'You creepy toad!'

Joseph: They said.

Brothers: 'Never in a million years will we **bow** down to you.
That's the last thing in this world that we would ever do.'

Joseph: Soon I had a second dream, which made me shout with glee.
Eleven stars, the sun and moon all **bowed** down to me ***(parents make sun and moon bow)***
The sun it was my father ***(father waves)***, the moon it was my mum. ***(mother waves)***
The stars they were my **brothers** and they **bowed** down, every one.
I found the dream so brilliant, I cried, 'Guess what I dreamt!'
And when my family heard it, they knew just what it meant.
My **brothers** raged ***(brothers shake fists)*** and even Dad ***(shakes head)*** could not share my delight.

Father: 'Me **bow** down to you?'

Joseph: He said.

Father: 'I don't think that is right.'

Joseph: After that my family seemed to go from bad to worse.
Each time my **brothers** saw me they'd stamp and spit and curse. ***(brothers stamp)***
They'd mutter and they'd threaten. They'd try to make me cow. ***(keep stamping)***
But I was strengthened by those dreams in which I'd seen them **bow**.
(stamping stops)
For deep down in my soul I knew that, though my dreams seemed odd,
They weren't imagination, they'd come to me from God.
So though my **brothers** clearly wished to tear me limb from limb,
I trusted God would change their hearts and I **bowed** down to Him. ***(Joseph bows)***

APPLICATION

Theme: God's sovereignty

Explore: Joseph

Joseph was his father's favourite son. He was the second youngest in the family and his mother, Rachel, was Jacob's favourite wife. He didn't make it easy for his brothers to get on with him (Genesis 37:2) – he comes across as being rather sneaky and boastful. Still God had chosen him for a special job.

Chat

Ask the group to imagine they are managing a world class football team and can choose any professional player they like as captain. Who would they choose? Say that choosing people for special roles is something God does. Chat about what was good about Joseph's attitude to being chosen and what was not so good.

Think

Remember what makes a job special isn't so much what the job is, as who that job is done for. Thank God that he gives each of us special jobs to do for him.

DRAMA 13

THE STRANGER

AGE 10+

SUBJECT: Reuben's guilty secret

BIBLE READING: Genesis 37:12–36

DRAMA NOTES:

Cast: Reuben, stranger.
Staging: Reuben is lying on a sleeping bag centre stage. Stranger comes over and shakes him.
Props: Sleeping bag, feather.

Stranger: Wakey, wakey, Reuben.

Reuben: ***(sits up groaning)*** Is it morning already? It feels like the middle of the night.

Stranger: It ***is*** the middle of the night. I've woken you up for a chat.

Reuben: ***(lies down again)*** But I want to sleep.

Stranger: Tough cookies. Keeping you awake is my job. ***(produces feather)*** If you won't chat I'll just have to tickle the soles of your feet.

Reuben: ***(sits up and draws his feet up)*** No… no… not my feet.

Stranger: So, you're ready to chat then?

Reuben: Oh, all right. What do you want to chat about? Who are you, anyway?

Stranger: Never mind that. I'm here to chat about your brother…

Reuben: Which brother? Simeon? Levi? Judah? I have… er… ***had***… eleven of them.

Stranger: I think you know which brother. The one everyone wants to chat about – especially the girls. The young, brilliant, good-looking one…

Reuben: Oh, Joseph. ***(lies down)*** There's no point talking about him. He's ***(sniffs)*** dead.

Stranger: Dead! A fit young man like that! What happened?

Reuben: It's so sad. ***(sniffs)*** The other day Father sent him out to the fields to see how my brothers and I were getting on. We're shepherds, you see. And a wild animal got him. We found his blood-stained robe on the way home. He must have been mauled by a lion.

Stranger: Funny – I heard a different story.

Reuben: ***(sits up)*** How do you mean ***different?***

Stranger: I heard that you and your brothers threw Joseph into a pit and then sold him as a slave to some passing traders.

Reuben: That's a lie! I had nothing to do with it. The truth is my brothers spotted Joseph in the distance and wanted to kill him. But I got them to put him in a pit instead. How was I to know they would go and sell him before I could get him out?

Stranger: So you're telling me you did your best to save Joseph – right?

Reuben: Right.

Stranger: And you're the eldest brother. The one who calls the shots.

Reuben: ***(puffs out his chest)*** Right.

Stranger: So if you were so keen to save Joseph, and if you call the shots, how come when the others started to talk about getting rid of him, you didn't just shut them up?

Reuben: Because… well… because… oh… if you must know Joseph was a total pain. Father thought the sun shone out of his eyeballs, and Joseph rubbed our noses in it, the little toad. I'd come down in the morning and it would be, 'Guess what, Reuben. I dreamt the sun, moon and stars bowed before me.' He meant US – his own family. I mean, can you imagine it – ME, the eldest brother, bowing to HIM!

Stranger: In other words the green-eyed monster made you do it. You were jealous of Joseph – so jealous you wanted him dead. And now look where it's got you. Joseph's out of your life but your father thinks less of you than ever, and that's without knowing what ***really*** happened to his favourite son.

Reuben: I've had enough of this. Just pack up your mind-reading kit and get out of my tent.

Stranger: ***(pushes Reuben back down)*** OK, OK no need to get worked up. We don't have to chat anymore if you don't want to. I'll sit here quietly at the bottom of your bed.

Reuben: ***(sits back up)*** No – I want you out of my tent. I want you GONE.

Stranger: Sorry, mate. I'm not going anywhere. I plan to stay with you for years and years.

Reuben: What? I don't understand. Who ***are*** you?

Stranger: Guess.

Reuben: No! ***(grabs stranger)*** Tell me!

Stranger: Well if you must know, I'm a guilty secret. Lots of people have them, Reuben, and I'm yours.

APPLICATION

Theme: Guilty secrets

Explore: Reuben

Reuben was the eldest of Jacob's sons, but he didn't have the strength of character to be a true leader. He went along with his brothers' plotting, instead of standing up to them. His father described him as 'turbulent as water' (Genesis 49:3-4) – the sort of person who gets swept into doing things he knows aren't right and feels ashamed afterwards.

Chat

What sorts of things keep you awake at night? What sorts of things help you to sleep? Look up 1 John 1:9. How might this verse help someone who can't stop feeling guilty. How could they put it into practice?

Think

Sometimes we're afraid of what would happen if people knew what we were really like. God knows us better than anyone – right down to the number of hairs on our head. He knows every wrong thought we've ever had; every wrong thing we've ever done; and he still wants to be our very best friend. Praise him for his forgiveness.

DRAMA 14

SIT, CROUCH, STAND

AGE 8+

SUBJECT: **God's plan for Joseph**

BIBLE READING: **Genesis 37:3–11**

DRAMA NOTES: This is an interactive drama with Joseph and the servant being played by leaders. The idea is that the children form the audience Joseph is addressing, and stand, crouch or sit/lie flat whenever he tells them to. At the appropriate points the servant introduces the different events, loudly and pompously. It is important that this should move fast, flowing from the servant's couplet introductions to Joseph's elaborations and back as smoothly as possible.

Cast: Joseph, servant.

Joseph: Thank you for inviting me to speak to you today. My name is Joseph and, way back in Old Testament times, I was Prime Minister of Egypt. Of course one of the great things about being a Prime Minister is that you get to travel to all sorts of different places. So here I am, with my servant ***(points to servant)***, in this strange century where a Pop Idol isn't a foreign god and Britney *Spears* isn't a dangerous weapon. And we have a *great* story to tell you.

Servant: ***(pompously)*** Don't think you'll hear it in your seat, for Joe will have you on your feet.

Joseph: It's true, I am going to ask you to stand up, because this story is a huge roller coaster adventure, packed with ups and downs. And like my servant said, we hope you'll come up and down with us. When things in my life are going great, I want you to stand up straight, when they're middling, you crouch, and when they hit rock bottom, you can sit or even lie flat on the floor. OK. Here goes. You're beginning on your feet, because my life starts really well.

Servant: The adventure of Joe's life, scene one – Joe is his father's favourite son.

Joseph: You get the picture. I'm the kid who has everything, including the latest gear in the form of a special multi-coloured coat. And then there are the dreams I have as a teenager. I dream all sorts of things bow before me and somehow I know those dreams are from God.

Servant: The adventure of Joe's life, scene two – Joe's brothers get into a stew.

Joseph: These dreams, along with the coat and some other stuff, don't go down well with my brothers. They hate the sight of me, and one day they do something about it.

Servant: The adventure of Joe's life, scene three – they decide that Joe should cease to be.

Joseph: So it's flat on the floor time. That day my jealous brothers strip me of my special coat, fling me into a pit and then sell me to some travellers who take me to Egypt.

Servant: The adventure of Joe's life, scene four – he's bought by Captain Potiphar.

Joseph: In Egypt I don't waste time moaning about what's happened. I work my socks off and you can get into crouching position now, because my efforts are rewarded.

Servant: The adventure of Joe's life, scene five – Joe becomes Pot's favourite slave.

Joseph: Potiphar puts me in charge of everything – his house, his fields. Things are going great… but don't stand up yet… because out of the blue it all comes unstuck.

Servant: The adventure of Joe's life, scene six – a lady lands him in a fix.

Joseph: Potiphar's wife tries to get me into bed with her and, when I refuse, she tells Potiphar I attacked her and he throws me in to jail. So we're flat on the floor again – right back to square one. But I keep doing my bit, which results in…

Servant: The adventure of Joe's life, scene seven – Joe interprets dreams in prison.

Joseph: Being able to explain what dreams mean is a gift God has given me. I end up explaining dreams for two prisoners – Pharaoh's chief cupbearer and his chief baker. And this leads to…

Servant: The adventure of Joe's life, scene eight – Joe tells the cupbearer his fate.

Joseph: I've good news for the cupbearer. I'm able to tell him he's going to get his old job back. In return, he promises to try and get me out of jail. So move back to crouching position. My hopes are high… but I'm in for another disappointment.

Servant: The adventure of Joe's life, scene nine – the chief cupbearer lets Joe down.

Joseph: It's back to the floorboards. The chief cupbearer comes out of jail and totally forgets me. OK, thump the floor. I felt like thumping it I can tell you. But, even though the future looks like me being stuck in jail for ever, God is at work.

Servant: The adventure of Joe's life, tenth scene – Pharaoh's troubled by a dream.

Joseph: Well, Pharaoh is troubled by two dreams actually – one about cows and one about grain. He so troubled he's *desperate* for someone to tell him what they mean... which is where God kick-starts the chief cupbearer's memory and he remembers how I helped him. Maybe you can guess what happens next...

Servant: Joe's life adventure, scene eleven – he's suddenly released from prison.

Joseph: On your feet, folks. This is it. I'm brought to the palace where God shows me that Pharaoh's dreams mean there are going to be seven bumper harvests followed by seven years of famine. I come up with a brilliant scheme to save grain. And before you can say, 'Praise the Lord!' Pharaoh's made me his Prime Minister. So stand on your toes, reach up as high as you can and then relax.

Servant: It's Joe's last adventure scene for now – he sees the world before him bow.

Joseph: And as I watch I marvel at the way God has brought this about; how he's been with me though all the ups and downs – using everything, even my jealous brothers, to work out his plans. So it's been great to meet you and thanks for joining in. And remember whether you're on top of the world or flat on your face, if you're living for God, He can work things out for you, too.

APPLICATION

Theme: Life's ups and downs

Explore: Dreams

Down through history, dreams have been one of the methods God has used to speak to people and get their attention. In the book of Genesis God speaks to Jacob in dreams (Genesis 28:12–15; 31:10–13.) He spoke to Joseph in two special dreams, when he was still a teenager, promising him that he would hold a high position. After many ups and downs, Joseph finally finds himself in this position of power. God used the chief baker's dream, the cupbearer's dream and finally Pharaoh's dream to bring about Joseph's promotion.

Chat

When we commit our lives to God, the deep longings and desires he puts in our heart can be like a dream for the future. Chat about your God-given dreams.

Think

Think about some of the ups and downs in your life. Right now, are you on top of the world, or flat on your face, or somewhere in between? Remember the secret of Joseph's success was giving his best even in the down times and trusting God to do the rest.

DRAMA 15

CEREAL STORY

AGE 9+

SUBJECT: Years of Plenty and Years of Famine

BIBLE READING: Genesis 41:46–49, 53–57

DRAMA NOTES: Suitable for reading in a group, or for performance at a harvest service.

Cast: Narrator, Mum Ricicle, Pop Ricicle, Coco Ricicle, Goldie Socks.

Staging: Narrator centre, standing in front of table covered with a full-length cloth round which the Ricicle family sit. The Ricicles should be wearing bathrobes with pillows stuffed up the front to make them look enormously fat. There are two or three large packets of cereal on the table and baking bowls and serving spoons in front of each family member. Goldie Socks is out of sight under the table.

Props: Table, floor length table cloth, different sized cereal packets, baking bowls, serving spoons, pair of yellow socks.

Narrator: Today we're going to visit Ancient Egypt where Pharaoh has made Joseph Prime Minister. God has shown Joseph that for the next seven years there will be bumper harvests. But these years of plenty will be followed by seven years of famine. Joseph has just ordered that all the extra grain should be collected from the fields and stored in the cities.

So now we're zooming in on the imaginary city of Cheeriopolis ***(moves to one side and continues speaking)*** where the Ricicle family is having breakfast. As always, Mum has poured out three gigantic bowls of cereal – but today something has gone wrong.

Pop: ***(looking into bowl)*** Someone's been eating my cereal!

Mum: Someone's been eating my cereal!

Coco: Someone's been eating my cereal ***(turns bowl upside down)*** and they've gobbled it all up. ***(starts to cry)***

Mum: Don't cry, Coco. It's been a bumper harvest. You can eat cereal till it comes out of your ears. ***(pours more cereal into bowl)***

Goldie Socks: ***(loudly)*** Oh no he can't!

Pop: ***(leaps up)*** Someone spoke.

Mum: ***(leaps up)*** Someone spoke from under the table.

Coco: Someone spoke from under the table and they're sitting on my feet. ***(Goldie Socks comes out from under the table. He/she should be wearing yellow socks)***

Ricicles: ***(together)*** Who are you?

Goldie Socks: I am Goldie Socks – a civil servant. I'm here to tell you that for the next seven years, no matter how good the harvest is, there'll be no more wasting the grain. All the extra is to be put into storage. ***(lifts giant cereal packet)***

Pop: What! You mean we won't be able to stuff ourselves with cereal any more?

Mum: Or let it go stale in our cupboards?

Coco: Or buy it just to collect the tokens from the boxes?

Goldie Socks: That's right. You will only be allowed to keep what you need.

(brings smaller packet out from under the table and sets it down)

Narrator: Well, when the Ricicles heard this, they were furious.

Pop: How dare anyone tell us we can't do what we like with our own grain.

Mum: We ought to be allowed to waste as much as we want.

Coco: I don't like you, Goldie Socks. You're mean.

Goldie Socks: Don't blame me. This is the Prime Minister's idea.

Narrator: But the Ricicles were so angry, they set upon Goldie Socks with their serving spoons and the poor servant was lucky to escape with his (her) life.

(Ricicles hit Goldie Socks with spoons and exit chasing him/her off stage – narrator moves centre stage)

Narrator: Seven years later, just as God had warned, the years of plenty came to an end and the years of famine began. There were food shortages everywhere – not just in Egypt, but in the surrounding countries too. When things got really bad, the Egyptians went and asked Pharaoh for food and of course Pharaoh sent them to his Prime Minister. ***(while narrator is speaking the table is cleared and Mum and Pop sit down at it. They no longer have pillows under their robes)*** And so it's back to the imaginary city of Cheeriopolis to see how the Ricicles are getting on. ***(narrator steps to one side)***

Mum: Oh, Pop, this famine is dreadful. I'm so hungry.

Pop: Have we any food left?

Mum: ***(pulls out a small variety packet, holds it to her ear and shakes it)*** Yes, yes, there's something here. ***(turns it upside down)*** A rice crispie – well, actually it's more of a rice soggy! Shall I divide it in two?

Pop: Let me see. ***(takes rice crispie and licks his lips, then hands it back to Mum)*** No, my dear. It isn't big enough to share. You can have the whole thing.

Mum: ***(sadly putting rice crispie back in packet)*** I think I'd better save it for Coco. He'll be hungrier than any of us when he gets home.

Goldie Socks: ***(off stage)*** Knock! Knock!

Pop: Who's there?

Goldie Socks: Noah.

Pop: Noah who?

Goldie Socks: ***(bounding in)*** Noah good place to eat?

Pop: But you're not Noah. You're that civil servant… Smallpox or Smelly Locks or…

Goldie Socks: Goldie Socks. I've come straight from the centre of town to bring you this. ***(produces box of Weetabix from under cloak)***

Ricicles: ***(grabbing it)*** Food! Food!

Goldie Socks: And there's lots more where that came from. Prime Minister Joseph has just opened the city storehouse and Coco has been helping distribute the supplies. People from all over the Middle East are coming to Egypt to get grain.

Mum: Oh, this is wonderful! What can we say?

Pop: Goldie Socks, we owe you our lives.

Golden Socks: Not to me you don't. We'd all be down to our last rice soggy if it wasn't for the Prime Minister. But he won't take the credit. He says we owe it all to God.

Narrator: And there we'll leave the Ricicles to their Weetabix. But let's remember that this is a 'cereal' story which means it goes on and on. In some parts of the world there are bumper harvests; in other parts there is famine. So if we have extra it's really important to try and share it round. That way more people will have enough.

APPLICATION

Theme: Not wasting resources or opportunities

Explore: Joseph's rise to power

In Joseph's day, Egypt was one of the world's most advanced civilisations. Pharaoh made Joseph his vizier – or chief minister. He gave him great power and a new name – Zaphenath-Paneah, meaning 'revealer of secrets' (Genesis 41:45).

During the years of famine, Joseph's family came to Egypt to buy grain (Genesis 42:1–3). At first they did not recognise Joseph – he'd been a teenager when they sold him and now he was almost 40. Joseph did not blame his brothers for what they had done (Genesis 45:5) and on their second visit he told them who he was. Then the whole family moved to Egypt, where the brothers looked after Pharaoh's herds and Joseph continued to rule for the rest of his life.

Chat

What sort of things can we waste? See how many different things you can think of e.g. food, water, time, money, opportunities. Make up a questionnaire with the title 'How wasteful are you?' Chat about ways in which we could improve.

Think

How often do I give up something so that somebody else can have enough?

PART TWO

LEADING ROLES

(The Good, the Bad and the Almighty)

DRAMA 16

ESCAPE FROM EGYPT

AGE 10+

SUBJECT: **Moses and Pharaoh**

BIBLE READING: **Exodus 7:1–7**

DRAMA NOTES: Suitable for group reading or performance.

Cast: Narrator, Pharaoh, Hebrew slave, Moses, Aaron, guard.
Staging: Narrator stage left, Pharaoh sitting on throne stage right, Hebrew slave leaning on brush.
Props: Brush, tooth brush, staff (for Moses).

Narrator: Over 3000 years ago Egypt was ruled by a very proud King.

Pharaoh: I am the ruler of Egypt. My name is Pharaoh.

Narrator: Pharaoh had made slaves of the Hebrews, God's chosen people.

Hebrew: I am a miserable Hebrew slave.

Pharaoh: Hey you, slave. Start brushing that floor.

Hebrew: ***(brushing floor)*** I wish God would get me out of here.

Narrator: God saw his people's misery and sent his servant Moses to talk to Pharaoh. ***(enter Moses and Aaron)***

Moses: I am M...M...Moses.

Aaron: And I'm Moses' brother, Aaron. Moses sometimes gets a bit tongue-tied so I'm here to help with the speeches.

Pharaoh: That's enough of the introductions. What do you two want?

Moses: Go on, tell him, Aaron.

Aaron: Moses says, God says, you have to let his people go.

Hebrew: ***(throws brush in the air)*** Whoopee!

Pharaoh: Let them go! Not likely. Slave, give me that brush.

Hebrew: ***(hands brush to Pharaoh)*** Yes, your Majesty.

Pharaoh: Now carry on sweeping the floor.

Hebrew: But you took my brush.

Pharaoh: So? Off you go and find another one. And if you can't find one, you can use your hands! I've been making life too easy for you, giving you everything you need to do your work. And Moses, you can tell the slaves who make bricks in the brickfields that, from now on, they can find their own straw.

Hebrew: ***(takes out toothbrush and gets down on his hands and knees)*** Pah! Thanks for nothing, Moses.

Narrator: Pharaoh thought he'd settled the matter, but Moses didn't give up.

Moses: Go on, tell him, Aaron.

Aaron: Pharaoh, Moses says, God says, you've got to let his people go… OR ELSE.

Pharaoh: Or else… what?

Moses: Or else there'll be… you know… tell him, Aaron.

Aaron: Or else there'll be TROUBLE.

Pharaoh: Oh, I'm soooo scared – NOT. Watch my lips. The Hebrews STAY PUT. ***(exit Moses and Aaron)***

Narrator: Pharaoh didn't really believe Moses' God could make trouble. He thought life would go on as normal. But the next morning when Pharaoh went down to bathe in the river Nile, ***(Pharaoh leaves throne)*** Moses was waiting for him. ***(enter Moses and Aaron. They stand beside Pharaoh. Moses stretches out his staff)*** Moses held his staff out over the river and next minute the water turned a murky reddish brown.

Pharaoh: ***(bends down, dips finger in imaginary river and sniffs)*** Prancing Pyramids! The water has turned into blood. ***(Pharaoh returns to throne)***

Narrator: In fact the water all over Egypt had turned into blood. Soon the whole country stank of dead fish.

Hebrew: Pooh!

Pharaoh: There's something fishy going on.

Aaron: We warned you there'd be trouble.

Moses: Now will you let God's people go?

Pharaoh: Watch my lips. The answer is 'N' 'O'... NO.

Narrator: So God sent a plague of frogs. ***(Hebrew slave and Aaron croak)*** There were frogs all over the place. In Pharaoh's bed... in his bath... in his breakfast cereal...

Moses: Now will you let God's people go?

(Pharaoh makes a croaking noise and shakes head)

Hebrew: He can't speak. He's got a frog in his throat.

Narrator: After the frogs came a plague of itchy little gnats that set the whole country scratching.

Moses: Now will you let God's people go?

Pharaoh: I will gnat.

Narrator: And so it went on. Pharaoh kept hardening his heart and God kept sending plagues. The plague of gnats was followed by a plague of flies. ***(Hebrew, Aaron and Moses 'ZZZZZ', Pharaoh swats round wildly)*** The plague of flies was followed by a plague of dead sheep and cows. ***(Hebrew, Aaron and Moses bleat, Pharaoh sticks finger in ears)*** The dead animal plague was followed by a plague of boils.

Pharaoh: ***(stands up)*** Oww. It's like sitting on barbed wire.

Moses: Now will you let God's people go?

Pharaoh: I'll boil in oil first...

Narrator: So the plague of boils was followed by a plague of hail. ***(Aaron, Moses and Hebrew stamp on floor. Pharaoh holds up arms to protect his head)*** which destroyed half the crops. Then came a plague of hungry locusts, which ate the other half up... ***(Aaron, Moses and Hebrew say 'gobble ... gobble ... gobble ...')***

Pharaoh: All right... all right... Moses, pray to your God. Tell him to end this plague and I'll let his people go.

Narrator: So Moses prayed and God blew the locusts into the Red Sea.

Pharaoh: Great! The locusts are gone.

Hebrew: Hurrah! I'm gone too.

Pharaoh: Not so fast, slave. You aren't going anywhere. I've changed my mind.

Narrator: Pharaoh went back on his word... and so the plague of locusts was followed by a plague of darkness. For three whole days there was no daylight in Egypt, except in the part where the Hebrews lived. By the time this plague ended even Pharaoh could see that Moses' God was alive and powerful. But still he refused to let God's people go.

Pharaoh: Moses, get out of my palace and never come back.

Moses: Very well, if that's the way you want it... ***(Moses and Aaron exit)***

Narrator: The stage was set for the tenth plague. While Pharaoh slept ***(Pharaoh snores)*** this plague stole silently across the whole land, striking every Egyptian family.

Guard: ***(runs on)*** Wake up, wake up, your Majesty. The whole land is in mourning. The eldest child in every household died during the night. All the firstborn children are dead – including your own son.

Pharaoh: My son! Oh no!

Guard: Please, your Majesty, please send the Hebrews away...

Pharaoh: Of course. That's the answer. I'll send them away this minute. I can't think why I didn't get rid of them sooner. Slave, tell Moses to get God's people out of Egypt... FAST.

Hebrew: You mean... you mean... we're ***free?***

Pharaoh: Yes... yes... you're free. Now GO. ***(exit slave)***

Narrator: Of course, no sooner did Pharaoh let his slaves go, than he began to have second thoughts...

Pharaoh: Summon my army. Jump to it. I want those Hebrews back. ***(exit Pharaoh and guard)***

Narrator: But Pharaoh didn't catch the Hebrews. Instead his army drowned in the Red Sea. So for poor proud Pharaoh the story came to a very soggy end, but for the Hebrews it was a new beginning. They set out with Moses for the Promised Land...

Hebrew: ***(off stage)*** We're free... yippee!... We're free... Praise God!

Narrator: ...full of praise for the mighty God who had freed them.

APPLICATION

Theme: God's power

Explore: Exodus

The book of Exodus is the second book in the Bible and tells how God brought his people out of Egypt (Exodus 1:1—12:30), led them through the desert (Exodus 12:31—18:27) and taught them how to live and worship him (Exodus 19:1—40:38). The Ten Commandments are found in Exodus 20:1–17.

Moses

Moses was one of the greatest leaders of all time. He grew up in Egypt and then spent years in exile in Midian before coming back to confront Pharaoh. He was a prophet (i.e. he brought God's Word to the people) and wrote the first five books of the Bible (known as the Pentateuch).

Pharaoh

The Egyptians called all their rulers Pharaoh. Pharaoh would have had a huge amount of power. He controlled the army and the religious life of his people, who believed he was a living god.

Chat

Most of the plagues did not affect Goshen, the part of Egypt where the Hebrews lived. On the evening of the tenth plague, each Hebrew family was told to kill a lamb and dab some of its blood onto the door of their home. Doing this meant their children were kept safe. Chat about how you think ordinary Hebrew families would have felt at this time. What would they have learnt about God?

Think

Get children to write down the most powerful thing they can think of. Write a praise prayer using their answers, e.g. 'We praise you God that you are stronger than x, more powerful than y' etc…

DRAMA 17

GOOD ADVICE

AGE 8+

SUBJECT: **Moses appoints Judges**

BIBLE READING: **Exodus 18:13–27**

DRAMA NOTES: This is an interactive drama involving the audience. Also suitable for group reading.

Cast: Narrator (adult), Moses, Jethro, two women – Jochim and Jael.
Staging: Opens with narrator centre stage, addressing audience.
Props: Desk, clipboard, scrolls, two cloaks, cue cards with list of complaints e.g. You stole my cloak… my staff… my bracelet; It's your turn to fetch water… tidy the tent… collect the manna; You promised to marry me.

Narrator: Imagine you have travelled back in time. You're part of a big group of Israelites waiting to speak to Moses. You're here because you and another Israelite have had a quarrel and you want Moses to settle it. So what you need to do now is get together with a partner. ***(children find partners)*** And the first thing you have to decide is what the quarrel was about.

Maybe it was about possessions. ***(hold up 'you stole my cloak/staff/bracelet' cue cards and get children to read them out)*** One of you is saying your partner stole something and your partner is denying it. ***(pairs role-play 'You stole my ______/Oh no I didn't/Oh yes you did' exchange)***

Or maybe it was about work. ***(hold up the 'it's your turn...' cue cards and get children to read them out)*** Swop round in your pair, so the partner says it's your turn to fetch the water or tidy the tent or collect the manna ***(NB be ready to explain what manna is if necessary)*** and you say it isn't. ***(pairs role-play 'It's your turn to______/Oh no it's not/Oh yes it is' exchange)***

Or maybe it was about relationships. ***(hold up the 'You promised to marry me' cue card and get the children to read it out)*** But we won't go there... The important thing is you're waiting for Moses. And here he is at last. ***(enter Moses)*** Good morning, Moses.

Moses: ***(sitting down at desk, and beginning to sort through scrolls without looking up)*** What's that? Oh yes... yes... good morning. I'm sorry I've no time to chat. There are so many people wanting me to make judgements.

Narrator: ***(consults clipboard)*** Before you start there's a gentleman to see you.

Moses: Tell him to wait his turn like everyone else.

Narrator: He says he's your father-in-law. ***(enter Jethro)***

Moses: Jethro! What brings you here? ***(he and Moses embrace)***

Jethro: I thought we could go train-spotting.

Moses: Train-spotting? But trains haven't been invented...

Jethro: I mean *camel* train-spotting. So what do you say?

Moses: Jethro, just look at the number of people out there. ***(points to audience)*** I can't leave them to go off and enjoy myself.

Jethro: So take a bit of extra time after lunch.

Moses: *Extra* time! That's a joke. I don't have *any* time. I just grab a manna-sandwich at my desk.

Jethro: Right. After tea, then?

Moses: Sorry, Jethro, but I'll be burning the midnight oil.

Jethro: You mean you're going to work through from morning to night without stopping?

Moses: That's about it. And now, I really must make a start on today's quarrels.
(Jethro stands back. Moses speaks to narrator) What's first?

Narrator: ***(consults clipboard)*** You could say it's a costume drama.

(enter Jochim, and Jael who is wearing two cloaks. They stand before Moses)

Moses: Well, ladies, what can I do for you?

Jochim: She took my cloak.

Jael: Oh no I didn't.

Jochim: Oh yes you did.

Moses: ***(to Jael)*** Madam, I can't help noticing that you are wearing two cloaks. Does one of them by any chance belong to Miss… Miss…

Jochim: Jochim's the name.

Moses: To Miss Jochim here?

Jael: The thing is, I took it as security when I lent her some money.

Moses: ***(unrolling scroll)*** Ah well... in that case, Miss er...

Jael: Jael.

Moses: Miss Jael... the Law is quite clear. This cloak is all Miss Jochim has to keep her warm at night. You should have given it back to her at sunset.

Jael: That's the Law, is it?

Moses: God's word says, 'If you take your neighbour's cloak as security for a loan, return it to him by sunset because his cloak is the only covering he has for his body.'

Jael: Well, if that's the Law... ***(she takes off second cloak and gives it to Jochim)***

Jochim: Thank you. ***(exit Jochim and Jael)***

Moses: One down... four hundred and seventy-four more to go...

Narrator: ***(consults clipboard)*** I make it four hundred and seventy-five...

Moses: ***(wearily)*** Next!

Jethro: ***(leaps forward waving)*** No, wait!

Moses: What's the matter? Why are you waving?

Jethro: Because I've just had a brainwave. The thing is, you can't go on like this. You're wearing yourself out. What you should do is appoint judges to help you. From each tribe, choose trustworthy people who know God's Law. Get them to sort out the simple quarrels. Then you'll only have to deal with the tricky ones.

Moses: Mmmm... yes... I see what you mean.

Narrator: I know I'm just the narrator but that sounds like a really great idea. Everyone will be seen more quickly.

Moses: OK. I'll talk to God and if this idea is from him, then that's what I'll do.

Jethro: Well said! ***(Jethro shakes him by the hand)***

Narrator: Well said, indeed. A wise leader isn't just able to give good advice; he's able to take it too.

APPLICATION

Theme: Good advice

Explore: Jethro

When Moses was still a young man he killed an Egyptian and had to flee from Egypt. He went to Midian where he met Jethro and married Zipporah, one of Jethro's seven daughters (Exodus 2:15-21). Moses and Zipporah had two sons, Gershom and Eliezer.
Although Jethro was not an Israelite, he was a worshipper of God and came to believe in the God of Israel.

Chat

Moses gets advice and guidance in two ways in this story. See if the children can work out what they are (from his father-in-law and from God's Law). Jethro advised him about a better way of coping with his workload and God's Law gave him the guidance he needed to judge court cases wisely and fairly. One of the things that usually sets good advice apart from bad advice is that good advice is given by people who want the best for us. Ask children to think who those people are for them? We can be absolutely certain that God only wants the best for us, therefore his Word contains the best advice of all.

Think

Thank God for people who give us good advice. Ask God to help us take it.

DRAMA 18

I SPY

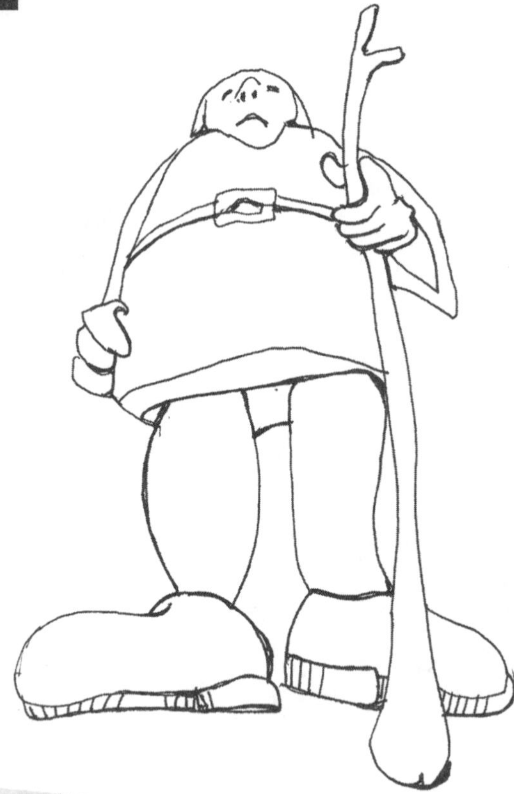

AGE 6+

SUBJECT: Twelve spies in Canaan

BIBLE READING: Numbers 13:1,2,27–32; 14:6,7

DRAMA NOTES: This is a simple action drama where the children follow the Narrator's lead. Beforehand the Narrator should set the scene, explaining how God had sent Moses to free the Israelites from slavery in Egypt and lead them into a land of their own.

Cast: Narrator.

Narrator: Moses said, 'Oh happy day,

See! Canaan is not far away. ***(point)***

I need twelve spies to lend a hand. ***(hold up 10 fingers and then 2 thumbs)***

by checking out the Promised Land.' ***(shade eyes as if looking into the distance)***

So he chose –
Shamua and Shapat ***(hold up a finger for each name)***
Igal and Palti
Gaddiel and Gaddi
Ammiel and Sethur
Nahbi and Geuel
Joshua and Caleb
and they all set off on a long, hot hike, ***(march on the spot)***
to find out what the land was like. ***(look into the distance)***

And when they got there they saw
rolling hills ***(make hill shape)***
leafy trees ***(make tree shape)***
juicy grapes ***(pick grapes)***
honey bees. ***(make buzzing sound)***

But what was this?
They also saw high walls ***(stand on tiptoes and stretch)***
round cities strong. ***(circular movement)***
And behind those walls lived the enemies of Israel – a mighty throng of Hittites
(children take up fighting positions and make punching movements)
Hivites ***(punch)***
Amonites ***(punch)***
Jebusites ***(punch)***
and enormous hairy Anakites. ***(children leap into the air like attacking lions)***

For forty days the spies looked round. ***(looking round action)***
Then back the twelve came, safe and sound, ***(marching on spot)***
to tell God's people what they thought. ***(hold chins, look thoughtful)***
Oh dear! It was a bad report ***(shake heads)***

Ten spies* said, 'The land is fair
(hold up ten fingers. *Leader may insert names of the ten)
but you should see the people there. ***(shake heads)***
Those giant hairy Anakites ***(show size of Anakites)***
will pulverize us Israelites.' ***(pulverising action with fist on palm)***

Still two spies* stood apart and cried,
(hold up two thumbs. *Leader may insert Joshua and Caleb's names)
'Remember God is on our side.' ***(point to heaven)***
'The tribes in Canaan may look tall, ***(shows size of tribes)***
but God is greater than them all.' ***(enveloping movement)***

Two spies had faith, while ten spread fear.
(two thumbs, praying gesture – then ten fingers, trembling)
Let's give the faithful two a cheer! ***(thumbs up and cheer)***

APPLICATION

Theme: Trusting God

Explore: Canaan

The land of Canaan, known as the Promised Land, wasn't very big, but it was full of fruitful trees and fertile valleys. The spies travelled from the south of the land to its northern tip and back – a round trip of around 500 miles.

Joshua and Caleb

Joshua and Caleb were the two spies who encouraged the Israelites to enter the Promised Land (Numbers 14:6-7). Their words fell on deaf ears and the Israelites ended up spending forty years in the wilderness. But God rewarded Caleb and Joshua for their faithfulness. After Moses died, Joshua led the Israelites into Canaan and there Caleb defeated the giant Anakites and captured the Anakite city of Hebron (Joshua 14:13–14).

Chat

Draw a figure on an OHP sheet and show how adjusting the lens on the OHP makes the figure bigger and smaller. Then imagine the figure is a problem. Chat about the sort of problem it could be and how problems seem bigger when we view them through the lens of fear and smaller when we look through the lens of faith.

Think

Children draw giant Anakites with pictures on their bodies of things they're afraid of. They screw the Anakites up and throw them in the bin as a reminder that God can help us do the same with our fears.

DRAMA 19

FAMOUS LAST WORDS

AGE 11+

SUBJECT: **Moses' Last Words**

BIBLE READING: **Deuteronomy 5:1–22**

DRAMA NOTES: Suitable for group reading or performance.

Cast: Lionel and Violet (presenters), Dan and Joe (teenage Israelites).
Staging: Presenters together at one desk, Dan and Joe beside them at another. (There may be red and green lights on the interviewees' desk, signalling when they are to start speaking. When the sketch begins, the light on the boys' desk is showing red).
Props: *(optional)* News Programme signature tune, CD player, red and green lights.

(signature tune)
Lionel: Good morning all. Welcome to Ancient Egyptian Network News. I am Lionel Locust.

Violet: I am Violet Viper.

Lionel: And for the next five degrees of the sundial we will be reporting live from the desert.

Violet: Picture the scene. Sand. Rocks. Thorns. And thousands of nasty Israelites.

Lionel: Yeah, there's one great sweaty sea of them all gathered to hear Moses. They've been knocking around this desert for 40 years, but now they reckon they're about to enter the Promised Land.

Violet: Of course we hope they'll forget their God and return to slavery in Egypt.

Lionel: And we've some breaking news for you. Soon they won't have Moses to keep them godly. The 120-year-old prophet may look chipper, but he's told the press his years of leadership are at an end.

Violet: Which makes *this* speech one of his last.

Lionel: So what are people saying? Can we tempt them to back to Egypt? Let's find out...

Violet: With us in the studio we have two young Miserableites, I mean Israelites... Dan and Joe. ***(red light on boys' desk off, green light on)*** Lads, what do you make of the show so far?

Dan: Well, it's just been basically Moses and the Ten Commandments.

Violet: ***(eagerly)*** The Ten Commandments. They're a *great* band!

Lionel: Vile, honey, the Ten Commandments aren't a band. They're... well... help me out here, guys.

Joe: They're the special laws God gave to Moses on Mount Sinai.

Dan: And today he's been reminding us to keep them.

Lionel: ***(sarcastically)*** Sounds like a bunch of fun!

Violet: So what do these laws say?

Joe: They say we should honour our parents.

Dan: Respect God's name.

Joe: Be faithful to the people we marry.

Violet: How quaint!

Dan: They also say we shouldn't lie, steal or murder.

Joe: Or bow down to idols.

Dan: Or have any other gods before the One True God.

Joe: Or work on his Holy Day.

Dan: Or think mean thoughts about people who have things we want.

Violet: Amazing! Whoever heard of a law about thinking! What do you make of that, Lie?

Lionel: Well, Vile sweetie, to me it all sounds pretty out of touch with today's world. I mean it's a good forty years since the Israelite's God suggested those commandments…

Violet: And times have changed.

Lionel: They sure have. So if you ask me, those commandments need updating. Just a little cut here. A get-out clause there. For example, 'No murdering' could become 'No murdering, except for folk you *really* hate…'

Violet: And 'No stealing' could become 'No stealing, except for things you really want.'

Lionel: And 'Honour your parents' could become, 'Honour your parents so long as they're not stupid'.

Violet: How do you mean, stupid?

Lionel: I mean stupid as in giving their kids totally dumb orders like 'go to bed now'. I mean kids should be free to do what they like. The laws Dan and Joe just recited haven't been changed for forty years.

Dan: Haven't been changed! We're not talking about socks here.

Joe: These are Laws for Living given DIRECTLY by our CREATOR.

Dan: Keeping them means the Promised Land and BLESSING.

Joe: Breaking them means no man's land and DEATH.

Violet: Boys, please, we don't use the D word on this programme.

Dan: Why not? It's a fact. People DIE. But the One True God has set before us a path of life. ***(green light off, red light on)***

Lionel: Cool it, guys! AEN listeners don't buy that kind of religion.

Violet: No, they certainly don't. And if this show hadn't been going out live that bit would have been cut.

Lionel: Yeah, sorry folks. By the sound of things Dan and Joe aren't going to see sense and go back to Egypt. But that's their lookout. The last thing we want to do is dump a load of superstitious religious claptrap on your civilised heads.

Violet: Especially when it's time for 'Look into the Future' with AEN astrologist, Lena Lizard.

Lionel: So right now we're going to play you out with a soothing little snake charming number. ***(signature tune begins)*** Just forget about the commandments and…

Violet and Lionel: Have a nice day.

APPLICATION

Theme: The key to blessing is knowing and obeying God's word

Explore: The Israelites

God told the Israelites to go into the Promised Land but they were too afraid to obey him (Numbers 14:26–35). A whole generation died in the desert. Forty years later God brought his people back to the borders of Canaan. Moses already knew that he would not be the one to lead the people into the land (Numbers 20:12). Instead he reminded them that knowing and obeying God's word was the key to future blessing.

The Book of Deuteronomy

The book of Deuteronomy records how Moses prepared the Israelites for what lay ahead, reminding them of what God had done and how he expected them to live.

Chat

True or false? People who hear and obey God's word are always healthy, wealthy and happy. People who hear and obey God's word can be sure of spiritual blessing (e.g. inner joy and peace). People who disobey God's word are more likely to run into problems.

Think

Spiritual check-up questions. Do you have your own Bible? How often do you open it? On a scale of one to ten, how hard do you try to remember and do what it says?

DRAMA 20

THE FIRST STEP

AGE 9+

SUBJECT: **Gideon**

BIBLE READING: **Judges 6:25–33**

DRAMA NOTES: Suitable for group reading or performance.

Cast: Reporter, Farmer Joe Ash, Mehetabel the Midianite, Zimri the Prophet, DI Shirley Holmes, PC Watson, Gideon.
Staging: Narrator stage left. Shirley Holmes seated at desk, centre stage, facing Farmer Jo Ash on other side of desk.
Props: Picture of foot with missing toe, desk, bell, rolling pin, cloak, sword.

Reporter: ***(breathlessly)*** Here we are in the unhappy Israelite town of Ophrah where the townsfolk keep getting attacked by Midianites and where local farmer, Mr Joe Ash, has just had his garden shrine wrecked by a mystery vandal. Late last night someone sneaked onto his land, chopped down the pole he'd put up to honour the Goddess Ashtoreth and smashed up his altar to Baal. The vandal then built another altar, stole one of Joe's bulls and sacrificed it to the Israelite God. So our story opens in the local police station where Detective Inspector Shirley Holmes is investigating this shocking crime. ***(reporter moves stage left)***

Detective S: Well Mr Ash, I'm glad to tell you our careful investigation is almost complete.

Farmer J: You mean whoever axed my pole, and altered my altar, and burnt my bull is about to be stoned to death?

Detective S: That's exactly what I mean. We now have the vital clue that will lead us to the culprit.

Farmer J: So what is the clue?

Detective S: It's a footprint, Mr Ash. ***(holds up foot)*** A footprint with only four toes – found in the dust at the scene of the crime. As you know my colleague PC Watson's inquiries have already led us to three suspects. So all we have to do now is find out which one of them has a missing toe. ***(rings bell)*** Watson, bring in Zimri the prophet. ***(enter Watson with Zimri the Prophet – stage right)*** Ah, good morning, Zimri. Has PC Watson explained why you're here?

Zimri: No.

Watson: Zimri is suspect number one. He's under arrest because he's against us Israelites building altars to foreign gods.

Farmer J: ***(seizes Zimri)*** Oh, so you think it's clever, do you, to axe me pole and alter me altar, and burn me bull and get us all into trouble with Baal? You're going to be stoned to death, you are.

Zimri: But... but... I didn't do it. I'm innocent.

Detective S: We'll see about that. Take off your sandal. We need to inspect your left foot.

Zimri: What! Are you going to cut off my foot?

Watson: Now there's an idea.

Farmer J: I've got a knife.

Detective S: No, no… that would stain the carpet, and anyway he might be innocent.

Zimri: I *am* innocent. ***(holds up bare foot)***

Detective S: Watson how many toes do you see?

Watson: ***(counts)*** One… two… three… four… five, Ma'am.

Detective S: Yes, I make it five too. Zimri, you can put your sandal back on again and go.

Zimri: I told you I was innocent. ***(exits)***

Farmer J: Well if Zimri the prophet didn't do it, who did?

Watson: I'll fetch the next suspect, shall I?

Detective S: Wait until I ring the bell… ***(Watson exits)***

Farmer J: So what are you waiting for?

Detective S: This is a dramatic moment. A moment of mounting tension…

Farmer J: For goodness sake, ring the bell…

(DS rings bell and Watson enters with glamorous Mehetabel the Midianite)

Watson: This is Mehetabel the Midianite. I brought her to the station because... well... because she's a Midianite and Midianites are always out destroying things.

Mehetable: But I ees not zee criminal. I ees married to an Izzraelite. And I ees a wooshipper of Baal. I say ooever destroyed hees altar deserves to die and eet definitely eesn't me.

Watson: So how do you explain the fact that you were spotted roaming the streets late last night carrying an offensive weapon.

Mehetabel: Zee weapon was zees rolling pin. ***(produces rolling pin from under cloak)*** I was walking 'ome after a baking party.

Detective S: A likely story. I say you had arranged to meet up with a band of Midianite raiders to attack Mr Ash's altar. Take off your sandal, please. I believe we shall find that one of your toes is missing.

Metetabel: I'll 'ave you know that every part of me is 'ere in zis very room. ***(takes off sandal – to reveal brightly painted nails. She wiggles toes)*** Zees little piggy went to market... zees little piggy stayed at 'ome... zees little piggy had roast beef...

Watson: All right... all right... that's enough. Ma'am, the suspect appears to have all her toes.

Mehetabel: And I 'ave all my 'air and all my teeths and all my...

Detective S: Yes... yes... We get the message. You may go.

Mehetabel: Byeeee! ***(Watson escorts Mehetabel off stage)***

Farmer J: Well, it looks like we're back to square one.

Detective S: We still have one final suspect... a young gentleman. Watson brought him to the station because he was spotted leaving your garden in the early hours of the morning. ***(shouts)*** Watson, bring in the final suspect.

Watson: ***(calls from off stage)*** You haven't rung the bell.

Detective S: ***(ringing bell)*** I have now.

(Watson enters with Gideon)

Watson: This suspect needs no introduction.

Gideon: Hiya, Dad.

Farmer J: But… but it's my son, Gideon. There must be some mistake.

Gideon: There's no mistake, Dad. Last night I tore down your altar to Baal, chopped up your Ashtoreth pole and offered a sacrifice to the Living God. I knew I was risking my life but I had to do it.

Farmer J: But… but why? You've always been such a quiet lad. I don't understand. What got into you?

Gideon: Dad, we've all been living in fear of the Midianites. But yesterday God sent an angel to say that I would conquer them. And then he told me to tear down the altar to Baal. I had to do it… it was like taking the first step…

Watson: The last step, you mean.

Detective S: Absolutely. Case closed. We have a confession. ***(rings bell)*** Take Gideon out and stone him to death.

Watson: ***(collars Gideon)*** This way, young man.

Farmer J: No… no… wait… what if he's right? I mean, if Baal has been offended he ought to be able to kill Gideon himself. And if Baal doesn't kill him, then maybe the One True God will use him to save us from our enemies.
(enter reporter)

Reporter: And that is exactly what happened. Gideon's bold action gave the Israelites an injection of spiritual backbone. After years of worshipping foreign gods, they turned back to the One True God and Gideon became a mighty warrior. ***(Watson takes cloak out from under desk and puts it on Gideon. Farmer J hands him sword)***

Detective S: ***(holds up foot)*** And here on sale to the highest bidder we have a historic impression of the mighty warrior's left foot!

Gideon: Look can we just settle this once and for all. That so-called clue of yours was a complete red herring. I had ten servants helping me tear down my father's altar. One of them may have left a print, but it certainly wasn't me.

Narrator: Which explains why the Bible doesn't make any reference to Gideon's feet. What it does tell us is that his act of obedience was indeed the first step to greatness. So forget the red herring, but remember the message. And whatever God calls you to do, be ready to take the first step.

APPLICATION

Theme: Spiritual growth

Explore: Judges

For about three hundred years after the Israelites went into Canaan they didn't have a King. Their leaders at that time were called Judges. In Canaan the Israelites found it hard to stay faithful to God. They worshipped other gods, became spiritually weak and were overrun by their enemies. Judges, like Gideon, called them back to the One True God and led them on to victory. The stories of this time are told in the Old Testament book of Judges.

Canaanite gods

The Canaanites worshipped a large number of gods, but Baal was the most important. In images he is usually seen holding a lightning bolt and he was believed to control the weather. Ashtoreth was the goddess of love and war. Farmers, like Gideon's father, were tempted to worship Baal and Ashtoreth because that was supposed to be the secret of a good harvest.

Chat

When Gideon is first mentioned in the Bible he is hiding from the Midianites, yet he becomes a mighty spiritual warrior. Chat about some of the things that can be a sign of spiritual weakness (e.g. being afraid of what other people think of you, not knowing what you believe). Then chat about things that are a sign of spiritual strength (e.g. confidence in God, influencing others in a good way). What kinds of things help people grow spiritually?

Think

Ask the children to draw outline footprints. In their print they can write one step which they think could help them grow spiritually in the week ahead.

DRAMA 21

THE BARLEY FIELD

AGE 7+

SUBJECT: **Ruth and Naomi**

BIBLE READING: **Ruth 1:22–2:12**

DRAMA NOTES: A harvest drama, suitable for group performance.

Cast: Narrators (ideally two – but the narration could all be done by one person), Ruth, Naomi, Boaz, a minimum of two people to play additional parts.

Staging: Narrators side by side stage right. Table with basin under it and chair, stage left.

Props: Apron (for Ruth), baby doll.

Narrator 1: Imagine a fine field of barley. The stalks are high and golden. The ears are full. There'll be a good harvest this year.

Narrator 2: ***(enter Ruth and Naomi stage left)*** But for these two women the future looks dark. Naomi and Ruth have just arrived in Bethlehem. Their spirits are low. Their purses are empty. They have no one to turn to but God.

Narrator 1: Naomi has spent the last ten years living in Moab. Her husband and her two sons died there. ***(Naomi sits down and mops her eyes)***

Narrator 2: Ruth was married to one of Naomi's sons. She left Moab to come back with Naomi – even though it would have been easier for her to stay in her own land. ***(Ruth sits at Naomi's feet)***

Narrator 1: Ruth has come with Naomi because she wants to help her. ***(Ruth pulls out basin, mimes washing Naomi's feet)***

Narrator 2: And because she wants to worship and serve Naomi's God.

Narrator 1: The two women are hungry but they haven't any money to buy food. ***(Naomi turns empty purse inside out)***

Narrator 2: ***(Ruth stands up)*** So Ruth decides she will go to the barley field and join other poor people who are out picking up the grain left by the harvesters. ***(Ruth moves centre stage)***

Narrator 1: Imagine the field now. ***(enter workers stage right)*** It is full of activity because the barley is being cut.

Narrator 2: The workmen are busy with their sickles and the women are binding the cut stalks into sheaves. ***(workmen and women mime cutting and binding)***

Narrator 1: Ruth feels nervous.

Narrator 2: She knows that people could turn against her because she's from another land. ***(workers point and whisper)*** She prays to God to keep her safe.

Narrator 1: Just then the owner of the field appears. ***(enter Boaz)*** His name is Boaz. Boaz notices Ruth and asks who she is. ***(Boaz talks to a worker)*** When he hears that this is the girl who came from Moab to help Naomi, Boaz speaks kindly to Ruth.

Narrator 2: He tells Ruth that she is very welcome to gather grain in his field and that he hopes she will come back. ***(Boaz talks to Ruth)***

Narrator 1: He tells the workers not to bother her and to let her drink water from their jug. ***(Boaz talks to workers – waves goodbye to Ruth, who waves back – and exits)***

Narrator 2: So Ruth stays in the field, ***(Ruth gathers grain)*** picking up stalks of fallen barley until the sun sets and it is time to go. ***(exit workers stage right. Ruth walks left across stage towards Naomi carrying apron as if it is full of grain)***

Narrator 1: Back home she tells Naomi about her day.

Narrator 2: And Naomi tells Ruth that Boaz, the kind man who helped her, is one of their relations.

Narrator 1: The weeks go by. ***(Ruth moves centre stage)*** Ruth keeps gathering stalks of barley and wheat in Boaz's fields until the harvest is over. ***(Ruth moves stage left)***

Narrator 2: Then Naomi tells her what to do next.

Narrator 1: Imagine a big open barn where Boaz and his neighbours have brought the sheaves that have been cut down from their fields. ***(enter farmers and Boaz)***

Narrator 2: There they beat the stalks with sticks to loosen the grain. ***(they beat grain)***

Narrator 1: Then they toss the stalks in the air so that the grain falls to the ground. ***(they toss stalks)***

Narrator 2: At night they sleep near the grain to make sure that thieves don't come along and steal it. ***(farmers lie down)***

Narrator 1: But one night, when the farmers are asleep, someone does creep into the barn. ***(enter Ruth)*** Ruth lifts the edge of Boaz's cloak and lies down at his feet. This is what Naomi told her to do. ***(Ruth lies down at Boaz's feet)***

Narrator 2: In those days, if a woman did that, it was a sign that she was asking the man to marry her.

Narrator 1: Boaz wakes up. ***(Boaz sits up)*** He is surprised and very happy to find Ruth at his feet. He knows she worships God and that she is kind and caring.

Narrator 2: He tells Ruth he will be glad to marry her. ***(Ruth and Boaz walk hand in hand towards Naomi, farmers follow clapping and exit stage left)***

Narrator 1: Imagine the barley field now. All the barley has been harvested. The field is empty and covered in stubble. ***(Ruth is given doll baby)***

Narrator 2: This is the field where one day Ruth and Boaz's little boy will run about and play. ***(Naomi, Boaz and Ruth with baby in her arms move centre stage)***

Narrator 1: Having a baby grandson has brought Naomi lots of joy. ***(Ruth hands baby to Naomi)*** She can see now how God has looked after her.

Narrator 2: Ruth and Boaz can see that God has looked after them too. They have sown seeds of goodness and faith and God has given a harvest of blessing. ***(enter Priest who takes baby from Naomi. Naomi, Ruth and Boaz put their hands together as if praying)***

Narrator 1: What they do not see is just how great that blessing will be. ***(Priest holds baby up as if praying for it)***

Narrator 2: For their baby, Obed, will have children of his own, and his children will have children and one of those children will grow up to be Israel's most famous King. ***(Priest hands baby back to Ruth)***

Narrator 1: Which goes to show that the blessings God plans for people are more amazing than we can ever imagine.

Narrator 2: And it reminds us to sow seeds of goodness and faith in our lives.

APPLICATION

Theme: Harvest. God's care and blessing

Explore: Ruth

Ruth came to Israel during the time when God's people were led by Judges. Her story is found in the Bible in the book called 'Ruth', which comes between Judges and 1 Samuel.

Boaz

The fact that Boaz was related to Naomi was very important. At that time in Israel the closest blood relative of a widow was expected to help and protect her and this included being ready to marry her. This is why, when Boaz finds Ruth at his feet, she reminds him that he is 'a kinsman-redeemer' (Ruth 3:9).

Chat

Draw pictures or diagrams to illustrate all the different kinds of caring that go on in this story (e.g. Ruth cares for Naomi, Naomi cares for Ruth, Boaz cares for Ruth and Naomi, Naomi, Ruth and Boaz care for Obed, the farmers care for the land, God cares for all). Chat about the way God uses people to show his care. With older groups a link could be drawn between how God cared for Ruth by sending Boaz, the kinsman-redeemer, into her life and how he cares for us by sending Christ, our Redeemer.

Think

Encourage children to think about people God has used to show his care, and thank him for them. Pray that he will help us show his care to others.

DRAMA 22

KING OF THE KITCHEN

AGE 8+

SUBJECT: **Samuel anoints David**

BIBLE READING: **1 Samuel 16:1–13**

DRAMA NOTES: Suitable for group reading or performance.

Cast: Two narrators, Sam.
Staging: The setting is an office. Sam is sitting behind a desk, with a telephone on top. Narrators side by side, stage left.
Props: Telephone, desk, chair, electric mixer, wooden spoon, carving knife (can be made out of cardboard with tinfoil covered blade), tray, four mugs, washing-up bowl.

Narrator 1: Sam, the Head Chef's assistant, is depressed. ***(Sam sits down on seat, head in hands)*** A heavenly banquet is being prepared in the kitchen next door – or at least it would be if the staff didn't insist on cooking their own way. ***(sound of breaking glass off stage – Sam puts fingers in his ear and shakes his head)***

Narrator 2: Sam had hoped that appointing Saul as manager would help to change things for the better, but instead Saul's refused to do what the Head Chef wants. So Sam has had to give him the sack.

Narrator 1: And now Sam's in really bad form ***(Sam slouches back again)***

Narrator 2: ...because he can't see any way of solving the problem.

(phone rings)

Narrator 1: ***(picks it up)*** Hello, Sam's office. Narrator speaking... ***(suddenly stands to attention)*** Oh yes... yes, he's here. I'll transfer you right away. ***(hands phone to Sam)*** Sam it's for you. It's The HEAD CHEF.

Narrator 2: ***(stands to attention)*** The Head Chef!

Sam: Good morning Boss... well, yes, I know I'm not acting as if it's a good morning... but I feel so bad about Saul... What's that? You want me to forget him and appoint a new manager. Today! Right now! But... but...Boss, I don't know where to start. Oh, I see. The sons of Jesse are waiting in the kitchen. So how will I know which son to choose? You'll show me their hearts. But *how?* Oh dear! He's hung up.

Narrator 1: Well this is a turn up for the menu. We're interviewing for a new manager.

Narrator 2: And the sons of Jesse are the candidates.

Narrator 1: So what are we waiting for? Bring them in.

Sam: No, listen! I don't want to speak to them directly. The Boss says I mustn't judge by appearances...

Narrator 1: So what will you do?

Sam: Panic! No, seriously… I'll ask each of the candidates to send me in an object that represents their hearts.

Narrator 1: That should be interesting. I'll go and tell them, shall I?

Sam: Yes, please. ***(exit narrator 1)***

Narrator 2: ***(peers after him)*** He's talking to Jesse's eldest son – a *very* impressive young man… tall… commanding… ***(enter narrator 1 with carving knife)***

Narrator 1: Jesse's first son, Eliab, has selected this knife. ***(brandishes carving knife)*** He says he'd make a steely manager – sharp and to the point.

Narrator 2: Nobody would mess with a manager like that.

Narrator 1: So what do you say, Sam?

Sam: ***(taking knife)*** I say no, Eliab isn't the one. He may be impressive but this knife tells me his heart is hard. We'll move on to son number two.

Narrator 2: ***(moves to the side of stage, calling)*** Next candidate, please. ***(returns waving wooden spoon)*** Our second son is Abinadab. He says he chose this wooden spoon because he's great at stirring folk to action.

Narrator 1: ***(peering off stage)*** He looks a real heart-throb too.

Narrator 2: So what do you say, Sam?

Sam: I say we don't need someone stirring things up just for the sake of it. ***(narrator 2 sets spoon down)*** Let's see what our third candidate has to offer?

Narrator 2: ***(moves to side of stage and calls)*** OK number three… we're ready when you are! ***(returns weighed down with electric mixer)*** Jesse's third son is called… ***(puts mixer on the desk, panting)*** Kenwood… I mean… Shammah.

Narrator 1: And?

Narrator 2: He says he's a wonderful mixer.

Sam: Which probably means he'd spend his whole time socialising and never get any work done. ***(narrators shrug and shake their heads)*** No, I don't think Shammah could manage the kitchen. In fact, I'm beginning to wonder if I'll *ever* find our new manager. How many more sons does Jesse have?

Narrator 1: ***(moves stage left and looks)*** I can see four. And by the looks of things they've all chosen the same objects. ***(comes back carrying a tray and four mugs)***

Narrator 2: Trying to soften us up with a coffee break, are they?

Narrator 1: ***(setting tray on desk)*** No. They each picked one of these... ***(picks up mug)*** to show how well they would... ***(displays handle)*** handle things.

Sam: Mugs! ***(buries his head in his hands)*** They chose mugs. The Head Chef doesn't need a mug for a manager. None of those four have got what it takes.

Narrator 1: ***(moves stage left and peers out)*** But, Sam... the kitchen's empty.

Sam: It can't be. There must be another candidate tucked away...

Narrator 1: The only son left out there is a kid.

Narrator 2: ***(peers out)*** About six inches smaller than all the others. He looks as if he's just come in from the fields.

Sam: Never mind what he looks like. We're not judging by appearances. Tell the lad I'm waiting to see into his heart. ***(exit narrators – they come back immediately with washing up bowl)***

Narrator 1: He says his name is David...

Narrator 2: ...and he picked this washing up bowl...

Narrator 1: ***(handing bowl to Sam)*** …because he's humble, empty and ready to be filled.

Sam: ***(punches the air)*** Yes! ***(holds up bowl)*** Friends, David will follow the Chef's instructions and clean up the whole kitchen. We've found our new manager at last.

APPLICATION

Theme: Doing God's will

Explore: Samuel

Samuel was the last Judge and a great Prophet. God first spoke to him when he was a young boy (1 Sam 3:3-12). Samuel helped select the first two kings of Israel, Saul (1 Sam 10:1-24) and David (1 Sam 16:1-13).

Saul

Saul ruled well to begin with and had many military victories but then he disobeyed God and as a result God no longer recognised him as King (1 Sam 15:10-29).

David

David was just a humble shepherd boy when God chose him to succeed Saul and sent Samuel to anoint him. He was not an obvious choice for a leader but God knew his heart (1 Sam 13:14). (A retelling of the story of Samuel anointing David may be found in *50 Five Minute Stories*, published by Children's Ministry.)

Chat

Play a trust game, e.g. children are blindfolded and guided through an obstacle course of chairs by partners walking behind them telling them which way to go. Each pair could be timed to see who completes the course fastest. Afterwards ask the group to say how they felt. Did those wearing blindfolds find it easy to do what they were told? Make a connection with the Bible theme: Samuel was like a blindfolded partner who trusted God to guide him and followed his instructions. Chat about some of the things that God sees and we don't.

Think

Give out paper cups. The children can copy out and decorate the words of 1 Sam 16:17, 'God looks at the heart', and stick them onto their cups. Pray with them that God would make us clean inside. Then fill the cups with juice.

DRAMA 23

ON THE RUN

AGE 10+

SUBJECT: **David in Hiding**

BIBLE READING: **1 Samuel 21:10–22:4**

DRAMA NOTES: Suitable for group performance or reading.

Cast: Narrator, David, King Achish, servant, supporter.
Staging: Narrator centre stage, holding large Bible to which he refers.
Props: Bible, pocket mirror, crown.

Narrator: Things have gone badly wrong for David. King Saul wants to kill him, so now he's on the run. ***(David runs on, and keeps running on the spot, looking anxiously over his shoulder)***

Narrator: He runs to the enemy city of Gath.

David: ***(stops running, out of breath)*** At least I'll be safe from Saul amongst his enemies.

Narrator: There, he gets spotted...

David: ***(whips out mirror and looks at his face)*** Oh no! As if things weren't bad enough already. I've got spots!

Narrator: I didn't say *spots.* I said *spotted.* There, he gets spotted by the servants of Achish, the king of Gath. ***(enter servant)***

Servant: I spy with my little eye someone beginning with 'D'. ***(narrator consults Bible)***

Narrator: ***(to servant)*** Shouldn't there be a few more of you?

Servant: There *should,* but the rest got stage-fright. They're hiding in the cloakroom*. ***(*refer to an appropriate room in your own building)***

Narrator: ***(rolling eyes)*** Carry on.

Servant: ***(marching up to David)*** I know who you are. You're David, the great Israelite warrior.

David: You can forget the great Israelite warrior bit. I'm on the run. Saul's trying to kill me.

Servant: ***(grabbing him)*** Forget the warrior bit? Not likely. We've a little saying here: 'Saul has killed thousands of our people, but David has killed tens of thousands.' I'm bringing you to King Achish.

Narrator: This gives David a nasty feeling.

David: What if King Achish looks for revenge? What if he takes me prisoner? Ohhh, I wish I'd never come here. My stomach is churning. My mouth is dry. My legs feel like jelly.

Servant: ***(knowingly)*** You've got stage-fright.

David: Don't be silly. My *life* is in danger.

Narrator: Yeah, those ninnies in the cloakroom* ought to get a grip. Stage-fright, indeed! At least David has a *right* to be scared.

David: ***(trembling)*** And I *am* scared. I'm scared witless. Hey, hang on a minute… that gives me an idea.

Narrator: It strikes David that one way to get round King Achish would be to pretend he has lost his wits.

(enter King Achish)

Servant: Look who I've got here, your Majesty. It's David, the great Israelite warrior who killed tens of thousands of our people. He's on the run from King Saul.

David: ***(drops onto all fours)*** Woof! Woof!

Servant: What's got into him?

David: ***(sits up and begs)*** Woof!

King Achish: I've got enough madmen around me already without *you* bringing another one into the house. That fool can't be David. ***(grabs servant and marches him off stage)***

Narrator: The plan works. David escapes from Gath and finds a new hide-out in Adullam's Cave. He's still on the run, and now as well as feeling scared, he feels humiliated. I mean, what a comedown!

David: A few months ago I had it all – fame, popularity, a brilliant future – and now look at me.

Narrator: In spite of this, deep inside, David knows he's not alone.

David: ***(kneeling)*** Have pity, God Most High! My enemies chase me all day. But even when I am afraid I keep on trusting you.

Narrator: Before long, God sends David company. His brothers and the rest of his family join him in the cave. Other people come too and soon David is the leader of 400 men.

David: ***(leaps up)*** Great! I've got over 400 supporters. ***(looks round)*** So where are they?

(enter supporter)

Supporter: We're right here, David. You can count on us. ***(to narrator)*** The other 399 got stage-fright. They're...

David: Don't tell me...in the cloakroom*!

Narrator: ***(rolling eyes)*** Of course, David still has his bad days, days when his stomach churns, his mouth goes dry, his legs turn to jelly and he feels like hiding ***(raising voice as if speaking to those off stage)*** *in the cloakroom**. But he doesn't. When fear wells up, *he deals with it.*

David: Lord God, I know for certain that you are with me. I praise your promises! I trust you and am not afraid. No one can harm me.

Narrator: No prizes for guessing the end of the story. ***(consults Bible)*** David doesn't get killed. Instead, he becomes king in Saul's place. ***(supporter puts a crown on David's head)*** It's a big relief for him not to be on the run any more.

David: ***(mopping brow and steadying crown)*** You can say that again.

Narrator: But he has learned some important lessons from those days when he feared for his life.

David: God used them to strengthen my faith.

APPLICATION

Theme: Dealing with fear

Explore: David

David was a shepherd boy when the prophet Samuel came and anointed him king in King Saul's place (1 Samuel 16:12–13). At first King Saul liked David and welcomed him to his court (1 Samuel 16:22), but later David's military victories and popularity made Saul so jealous, he wanted David dead (1 Samuel 19:8–10). All through his life, even when he was in the cave of Adullam, David wrote songs and prayers. You can read his words from the cave in book of Psalms (Psalm 142). In this Psalm David is honest about his feelings but it is clear that his faith gives him courage and strength.

Chat

Visit the Voice of the Martyrs website, www.vom.org, for up-to-date information on Christians whose lives are in danger today. What can we learn from these Christians? What can we do to help them?

Think

Everyone has to deal with fear – and no kind of fear is unimportant to God. Give each child a piece of playdough which should be rolled into a ball. Ask them to think of the things they're afraid of right now... maybe stuff going on at home or at school. Pass round a box of drawing pins (carefully supervised, of course) and tell them to pick out one drawing pin to represent each fear. Read Psalm 142. Encourage children to hand their fears over to God, as they stick their pins into the dough.

DRAMA 24

A COLOURFUL TALE

AGE 6+

SUBJECT: **Elijah at the brook**

BIBLE READING: **1 Kings 17:1–9**

DRAMA NOTES: A simple drama for young children who can wave different coloured ribbons or crêpe paper streamers as the verses are being read.

Cast: Narrator, 5+ children to wave ribbons or streamers.
Props: Black, brown, red, white, blue, gold and green ribbons or crêpe paper streamers.

Narrator: King Ahab had a hard *dark* heart. ***(children wave black ribbons with a whipping motion)***
He'd been a bad king from the start.
So to his court a prophet came.
Elijah was the prophet's name.
God's word blazed from him like a flame,
saying there'd be no more rain.

Soon the earth was *brown* and dry.
(wave brown ribbons at foot level)
Cows and sheep began to die.

Ahab got mad. His face went *red*.
(wave red ribbons in a circular motion)
'This is Elijah's fault,' he said.
'So hunt him down. I want him dead.'

'Help, Lord!' Elijah's face went *white.*
(wave white ribbons in a circular motion)
But God had plans to put things right.
He led Elijah to a brook,
where no-one else would think to look.

Next thing *black* birds came flying by,
(wave black ribbons overhead)
delivering a food supply.
White was the bread and *red* the meat
(wave red and white ribbons at foot level)
they dropped down at the prophet's feet.
Blue was the water in the stream
(wave blue ribbons at foot level)
that kept Elijah safe and clean.

And then one day the brook turned *brown*.
(wave brown ribbons at foot level)
Elijah looked up with a frown.
'Lord,' he said. 'There's something wrong.
'I'm still here, but the water's gone.'

God smiled. The smile of God is *gold*.
(wave gold ribbons overhead)
He said, 'A widow has been told
to open up her home to you.
Now go and see what I will do.'

Elijah went. He proved God's power.
Each month, each week, each day, each hour
God kept him safe till he sent rain
and all the fields turned *green* again.
(wave green ribbons in a circular motion)

And so the *colours* in this tale
(wave all colours at all levels)
remind us God will never fail.
His love is deep. His mercy's wide
and we can trust him to provide.

APPLICATION

Theme: God's provision

Explore: Ahab

King Ahab was the eighth king of Israel and a real Bible baddie. His wife Jezebel talked him into building a Temple to Baal in Samaria, the capital city of the Northern Kingdom (1 Kings 16:32). All through his life Ahab only listened to prophets who told him what he wanted to hear. Prophets like Elijah, who spoke the truth, were persecuted and flung into jail. In the end, Ahab's habit of listening to the wrong people led to his death on the battle-field (1 Kings 22:1-40). (This story is retold in *50 Stories for Special Occasions*, published by Children's Ministry.)

Elijah

Elijah is one of the most famous Old Testament prophets. The drought, which he prophesied, went on for three years and ended in a mountain-top clash between him and the prophets of Baal (1 Kings 18). There God clearly showed his power.

Chat

Under the heading 'God Provides', use pieces of coloured crêpe paper to make a collage of Elijah by the brook. Chat about how Elijah would have felt when the brook dried up. What did he do? Chat about the different ways in which God provides for us.

Think

Ask the children to imagine a conversation between God and a raven, when He tells it to take meat and bread to Elijah. Use an old black sock to make a raven glove puppet and act the conversation out.

DRAMA 25

TOP GOD

AGE 8+

SUBJECT: **Daniel in the Lions' Den**

BIBLE READING: **Daniel 6:25–27** (to be read after drama)

DRAMA NOTES: Suitable for group reading or performance.

Cast: Narrator 1, Narrator 2, King Darius, Daniel, Advisor 1, Advisor 2, guards, lions. (The cast can be reduced to 6 by having a single narrator and one guard, and by asking the audience to roar when they hear the word 'lions'.)
Staging: King Darius centre stage, Narrator 1 and Advisors 1 and 2 stage left, Narrator 2 and Daniel stage right.

Narrator 1: King Darius was King of Babylon.

Narrator 2: Being king meant making lots of decisions and Darius had three special advisors to help him. One of these advisors was Daniel. ***(Daniel approaches the King)***

Daniel: ***(bowing)*** Good afternoon, your Majesty. You wished to see me.

King: Yes, indeed Daniel. I wanted to tell you how pleased I am with your work. I'm thinking of making you my chief advisor. ***(Daniel and King exit stage right)***

Narrator 1: This made the other two advisors very jealous.

Advisor 1: Did you hear the latest? The King's about to give goody-goody Daniel the top job in the land.

Advisor 2: No way. We've got to stop him.

Narrator 2: So they watched Daniel, trying to catch him breaking the law so they could get him into trouble. ***(Daniel enters, walks round the stage while advisors watch closely)***

Narrator 1: They watched him for days, but Daniel did nothing wrong. The only thing they noticed was that every day Daniel would kneel beside his window and pray to God.

Daniel: ***(kneeling)*** I praise you God – Mighty King – Ruler of all the earth.

Narrator 2: This gave the jealous advisors an idea. They suddenly thought of a way to get Daniel eaten up.
(lions appear momentarily stage left, roar and disappear again. Advisors exit stage right. Daniel remains kneeling)

Narrator 1: The two advisors went to King Darius and talked him into making a law that said people could only pray to him. ***(enter advisors and Darius stage right)***

Narrator 2: Anyone caught praying to any other god would be thrown to the lions.

(lions appear stage left – roar – and disappear)

Narrator 1: King Darius liked this law.

King: It's a brilliant law!

Narrator 2: Of course King Darius never thought how this brilliant new law would affect his good friend Daniel. ***(King Darius shakes hands with advisors and exits stage right. Advisors walk over to Daniel)***

Advisor 1: Daniel, we've got some news for you. There's a new law. A law about praying. ***(Daniel stands up)***

Advisor 2: That's right. For the next thirty days, people can only pray to King Darius. He's top god. If you pray to any other god, you're dead.

Narrator 2: Guess what Daniel did when he heard that? He went right home, knelt beside his window and started praying to the One True God. ***(Daniel kneels, while advisors watch)***

Daniel: I praise you God – Mighty King – Ruler of all the earth.

Narrator 1: The jealous advisors could hardly wait to get to the palace. ***(Daniel exits stage left. King Darius enters stage right)***

Advisor 1: ***(panting)*** We've found someone, King. We've found someone who won't obey your law.

Advisor 2: What do you want us to do with him?

King: Bring him to me and then I'll have him thrown to the lions! ***(lions appear – roar – and disappear. Advisors fetch Daniel)***

Advisor 1: Here is the man. Here is your law-breaker.

Daniel: ***(bowing)*** Good evening, Your Majesty

King: Oh no. Not you, Daniel. You are my friend. I don't want to put you to death.

Advisor 1: But you must, your Majesty.

Advisor 2: The law is the law, your Majesty. It cannot be broken.

King: I have no choice. Guards, take Daniel away. ***(guards march Daniel stage left)*** No... wait I'm coming too... ***(King and advisors follow)***

Narrator 1: King Darius went with Daniel to the mouth of the lions' den. ***(lions roar but don't appear)***

Guards: In you go, Daniel. Into the den with you. ***(Daniel is pushed off-stage)***

King: Oh dear! Those lions sound very hungry. Daniel I'm so sorry about this. I really hope your God will rescue you...

Guards: Excuse us, your Majesty. We just need to roll this stone across the entrance... ***(pull screen across)*** we don't want those lions escaping.

Advisor 1: You mean we don't want Daniel escaping.

King: I feel dreadful. I never meant this to happen. It's all been a terrible mistake.

Narrator 2: King Darius went home to his palace and didn't sleep a wink all night as he thought of Daniel being chewed up. ***(King and advisors move stage right, guards stand in front of screen)***

Narrator 1: First thing in the morning he ran down to the den. ***(King runs centre stage, advisors follow)***

King: ***(to guards)*** Move the stone! ***(guards move screen)*** My friend, Daniel, are you alive? How are you?

Daniel: ***(calls from off-stage)*** Alive and well, your Majesty.

King: Thank goodness!

Narrator 2: Yes, Daniel was completely unharmed. ***(guards bring Daniel out and King hugs him)***

Narrator 1: He'd spent the whole night with a bunch of starving lions and they couldn't even lick him. God had sent an angel to shut their mouths. ***(lions appear, making stiffled roaring noises, then disappear)*** It was a miracle and it taught King Darius a thing or two.

King: Daniel's God is the real Top God. I should never have listened to those other two advisors. Guards, throw them to the lions!

Advisors: No! No! Help! Argh! ***(guards throw advisors off stage, lions roar loudly, screen is pulled back. King and Daniel move to the front of stage)***

Narrator 1: Then the King went back to his palace and made another law.

King: From now on everyone in this kingdom is to follow Daniel's God. ***(King Darius and Daniel kneel down side by side in an attitude of prayer)***

Narrator 2: So our story ends with Daniel at peace.

Narrator 1: And his enemies in pieces. ***(lions roar)***

Narrator 2: And King Darius worshipping the real Top God.

APPLICATION

Theme: Helping friends learn about God

Explore: Daniel

When Daniel was a teenager, the Babylonians attacked Jerusalem, destroyed the Temple, captured some of the people and took them off to Babylon. (It was at this time that the Israelites from Judah became known as Jews.) Daniel was one of those who was taken away. Despite being so far from home, he stayed faithful to God. He was a prophet and his prophecies are written down in the Old Testament Book of Daniel. Daniel's wisdom and his ability to interpret dreams meant that he rose to a high position in Babylon. His escape from the lion's den happened when he was 80 years old.

Chat

About friends and what makes a good friend. Then ask what it was about Daniel that made the King think of him as a friend? How did that friendship help the King learn about God?

Think

Bring in craft materials for children to make invitations to their children's club or church group. Suggest that each child takes an invitation and aims to invite one friend who isn't involved in church to come along so they can learn more about God.

DRAMA 26

BEHIND THE MASK

AGE 9+

SUBJECT: **Nehemiah**

BIBLE READING: **Nehemiah 2:1–9**

DRAMA NOTES: Suitable for performance or group reading.

Cast: Narrator, Nehemiah, King Artaxerxes, Hanani, servants (2+).
Staging: Servants and Nehemiah in a line – centre stage, narrator – stage right, chair – stage left.
Props: Smiling paper plate masks on sticks for Nehemiah and servants, paper plate mask for King – frowning face one side, smiling face on the other, chair, goblet-style cup.

Narrator: ***(points to servants who hold up masks)***
Artaxerxes, King of Persia, had made a rule in court.
His servants must look happy, no matter what they thought.
No one should look impatient. No one should look annoyed.
In the presence of their King they must look overjoyed.

(servants lower masks)

Servant 1: My feet are killing me. I just can't do it anymore. I can't keep smiling.

Servant 2: Me neither. My head's splitting.

Nehemiah: Come on, you two. You know as well as I do that the King expects service with a smile. If he doesn't get it you could lose your heads.

Servant 1: Watch out. He's coming.

Nehemiah: Quick. *Smile!*

(enter Artaxerxes stage left, holding up mask frowning side out – servants hold up smiling faces – Artaxerxes sits on throne, looks at servants and turns his own mask to smiling face)

King: Nehemiah, bring me my wine.

Nehemiah: ***(takes cup to King, holding up mask)*** Here you are, your Majesty.

King: Excellent. ***(sips wine)*** And now, Rebus and Pison, as a special treat you may come and listen to me practising my flute. Nehemiah, your brother Hanani has just arrived from Jerusalem. I'll leave you with him to catch up on the latest news.

Nehemiah: Thank you, your Majesty. ***(exit King and servants)***

Narrator: As Nehemiah waited, he thought about the past,
And how the Jewish people were going home at last.
For though he lived in Persia, Nehemiah was a Jew –
He loved and served the One True God. He served the King well too.

(enter Hanani)

Nehemiah: Hanani, it's great to see you. Tell me, how are things back home in Jerusalem?

Hanani: Not good, I'm afraid. The city walls are in ruins and the Jews that have returned there just seem to have given up.

Narrator: Oh dear! The news Hanani brought made Nehemiah weep.
Jerusalem's gates were burnt. The city walls lay in a heap.

Nehemiah: This is terrible. There must be something we can do.

Hanani: I'm sorry brother, but the situation really seems hopeless. And now I must be off. Perhaps I will have better news about the city walls next time, but I doubt it.

Nehemiah: Goodbye, my brother. God be with you. ***(exit Hanani)***
I must talk to God about this.

Narrator: Nehemiah went into his room, his shoulders bowed in pain.
He longed that God would show him how to build those walls again.
For days he wept and prayed aloud. He didn't eat a thing.
He knew one man alone could help – Artaxerxes, the King.

Nehemiah: ***(stands up)*** I must tell the King about this. He alone has the power to see that Jerusalem's walls are rebuilt…

Narrator: But how could Nehemiah hope to bring the subject up
when all he did was bow and smile and hand the King a cup?

Nehemiah: There's nothing else for it. I'll have to stop pretending to be happy.
I must let the King see how upset I am – even if it costs me my life.

(enter servants – who line up as at the beginning)

Servant 1: Quick Nehemiah, get into line. The King's on his way to the throne room.

Servant 2: My head's still splitting.

Servant 1: Put your smiley face on. You know your life depends on it.

(servants hold up smiley faces – Nehemiah doesn't. Enter King)

Servants 1 & 2: ***(to Nehemiah)*** For goodness sake – *smile!*

Narrator: The King sat down upon his throne and called out for his wine...

King: Nehemiah, bring me my wine.

Narrator: ...But for once his servant didn't act like everything was fine.
He didn't wear a happy face. He wore a frown instead.
In short he set out on a course that could have left him dead.

(Nehemiah approaches King and hands him his cup)

King: What's this, Nehemiah. You aren't smiling! You dare to look sad in my presence.

Servant 1: It's suicide.

Servant 2: I can't bear to watch.

Narrator: As Artaxerxes raised his voice, the servants held their breath.
They knew that Nehemiah stood one smile away from death.
Then Artaxerxes gave a shrug. God's spirit kept him calm.
He reached out to Nehemiah and took him by the arm.

King: You've always been a good, loyal servant to me, Nehemiah. And I can see you are troubled. Please tell me what's wrong.

Nehemiah: It's the city of Jerusalem, my King. My parents are buried there and it's in ruins.

King: But what can I do about this?

Nehemiah: You could give me permission to travel home to Judah and help rebuild the city walls.

Narrator: To everyone's amazement, the King didn't answer no.
God's spirit kept on working till he murmured –

King: You may go.

Narrator: Nehemiah's sad look vanished. A beam came in its place.
(Nehemiah smiles)

Nehemiah: Oh thank you, your Majesty. Thank you so much.

Narrator: Yes. Nehemiah left that day with a BIG smile on his face.
(servants and King clap as Nehemiah exits smiling)

APPLICATION

Theme: Hiding feelings

Explore: Jerusalem

In 586 BC the city of Jerusalem fell to the Babylonians and the Jewish people were carried off into exile. Jeremiah prophesied that after 70 years God would bring his people back from exile (Jeremiah 29:10), and this prophecy was fulfilled when the Persian king Cyrus II conquered the Babylonian empire. The return from exile and the rebuilding of Jerusalem went on for over 100 years, but in 445 BC, when Hanani came to see Nehemiah, it had hit a major set-back.

Nehemiah

As the King's cupbearer, Nehemiah had the job of tasting the King's wine to make sure it wasn't poisoned. It took him four months to travel from Susa (King Artaxerxes' winter capital) to Jerusalem. Soon after his arrival, he was appointed Governor of Judah and he stayed there for another 12 years. Under his leadership the wall around Jerusalem was rebuilt in 52 days. You can read Nehemiah's story in the Bible, in the book of Nehemiah.

Chat

Let everyone make smiley masks, then chat about times when we wear a smiling mask to hide our true feelings. (Examples could be acted out as role plays.)
What sort of things upset us? Do we ever get upset the way Nehemiah did when we see things going on that don't please God?

Think

Ask the children to think of someone who often wears a smile but underneath they know they are having problems. Pray for them – especially that God will help them find the right people to talk to.

PART THREE

STAR PART

(From the Manger to the Throne)

DRAMA 27

COUNTDOWN TO CHRISTMAS

AGE 8+

SUBJECT: Jesus – the Promised Saviour

BIBLE READING: Luke 2:1-14

DRAMA NOTES: This rhythmic drama is designed for performance by a children's group at Christmas. If possible the Bible verses should be displayed on screen. Alternatively they could be read by an adult reader.

Cast: A minimum of three children. Could involve up to seventeen.
Optional cast members: Adam, Eve, Abraham, Jacob, Pharaoh, slave, Moses, two Israelites, King David, Isaiah, Roman soldier, Mary, Joseph.
Staging: Child 1 reads the narrative couplets. Child 2 moves the hour hand on a cardboard clock face (or mimes the movement using their own arm). Child 3 uses a percussion instrument to make the sound of a ticking clock. The drama opens with child 2 centre stage, with empty manger to one side. Child 1 and adult narrator (if used) stage right. Child 3 stage left.
Props: Large cardboard clock face, with moveable hand (optional), crown, map showing Canaan, signs saying 'Home Sweet Home', 'Kings Rule OK' and 'This King will reign forever', percussion instruments to make sounds of ticking clock and chiming bells, manger.

Child 1: God spoke the word, and time began.
(child 3 begins ticking sound with four beats before child 1 says the next line. Ticking then continues throughout the drama. Child 2 holds up clock with hand at twelve o'clock position)
He made the world and then made man. ***(enter Adam and Eve)***

Accompanying words: (projected onto a screen or read by an adult narrator) *Genesis 1:27* So God created man in his image; in the image of God he created him: male and female he created them.

Child 2: One o'clock. ***(clock hand moved to one o'clock position)***

Child 1: But early in the course of time, people ruined God's design.

(Adam and Eve mime eating forbidden fruit as child 1 speaks)

Accompanying words: *Genesis 3:6* When the woman saw that the fruit of the tree was good for food and pleasing to the eye, and also desirable for gaining wisdom, she took some and ate it. She also gave some to her husband who was with her and he ate it.
(Adam and Eve step back behind the clock)

Child 2: Two o'clock. ***(clock hand moved to two o'clock position – enter Abraham)***

Child 1: So God chose faithful Abraham to start his great salvation plan.
(Abraham mimes kneeling down and praying as child 1 speaks)

Accompanying words: *Genesis 18:17,18* Then God said, 'Shall I hide from Abraham what I am about to do? Abraham will surely become a great and powerful nation and all nations on earth will be blessed through him.'

Child 2: Three o'clock. ***(clock hand moved to three o'clock position. Abraham steps back. Enter Jacob)***

Child 1: God vowed to bless Abe's family line and give them Canaan as a sign.
(Jacob holds up map and points to Canaan)

Accompanying words: *Genesis 35:11a,12* And God said to (Jacob)… 'The land I gave to Abraham and Isaac I also give to you, and I will give this land to your descendants after you.'

Child 2: Four o'clock. ***(clock hand moved to four o'clock position. Jacob steps back. Enter Pharaoh leading chained slave)***

Child 1: Before this promise came to be God's people suffered slavery. ***(slave mimes building)***

Accompanying words: *Exodus 1:8a,11* Then a new king… came to power in Egypt. 'Look,' he said to his people, 'the Israelites have become much too numerous for us…' So they put slave masters over them to oppress them with forced labour.

Child 2: Five o'clock. ***(clock hand moved to five o'clock position. Enter Moses)***

Child 1: In time, God stopped his people's woe. Moses made Pharaoh let them go. ***(Moses makes Pharaoh release slave. Pharaoh steps back)***

Accompanying words: *Exodus 3:10* (The Lord said to Moses) 'Now, go. I am sending you to Pharaoh to bring my people, the Israelites, out of Egypt.'

Child 2: Six o'clock. ***(clock hand moved to six o'clock position. Enter two more Israelites)***

Child 1: For forty years the tribes did roam, ***(additional four beat pause as Moses, ex-slave and Israelites mime walking)*** until God led them to their home.

Accompanying words: *Psalm 78:52,55* (God) brought his people out like a flock; he led them like sheep through the desert… He drove out nations before them; he settled the tribes of Israel in their homes. ***(Moses and ex-slave step back. First Israelite holds up sign saying 'Home Sweet Home')***

Child 2: Seven o'clock. ***(clock hand moved to seven o'clock position. Israelites mime working in fields)***

Child 1: At first they did what judges said, but soon they asked for kings instead. ***(second Israelite holds up a sign saying 'Kings Rule OK')***

Accompanying words: *Acts 13:20, 21* After this God gave them judges until the time of Samuel the prophet. Then the people looked for a king and he gave them Saul son of Kish, who reigned for forty years.

Child 2: Eight o'clock. ***(clock hand moved to eight o'clock position. Enter King David, carrying crown)***

Child 1: Some kings were bad, some kings were good. King David ruled just as he should. ***(David puts on crown. Two Israelites step back)***

Accompanying words: *Acts 13:22* After removing Saul, (God) made David their king. He testified concerning him, 'I have found David son of Jesse a man after my own heart, he will do everything I want him to do.'

Child 2: Nine o'clock. ***(clock hand moved to nine o'clock position. David steps back. Enter Isaiah)***

Child 1: But God had promised something more – A King who'd be a true saviour. ***(Isaiah holds up sign saying 'This King will reign forever')***

Accompanying words: *Isaiah 9:6–7b* He will be called Wonderful Counsellor, Mighty God, Everlasting Father, Prince of Peace. Of the increase of his government and peace there will be no end. He will reign on David's throne and over his kingdom… from that time on and for ever.'

Child 2: Ten o'clock. ***(clock hand moved to ten o'clock position. Isaiah steps back. Enter Roman soldier)***

Child 1: This promise was a ray of light to Jews now crushed by Roman might. (***Roman soldier marches up and down)***

Accompanying words: *Luke 2:1* In those days Caesar Augustus issued a decree that a census should be taken of the entire Roman world. And everyone went up to his own town to register.

Child 2: Eleven o'clock. ***(clock hand moved to eleven o'clock position. Soldier steps back. Enter Mary and Joseph)***

Child 1: At last the hour had almost come. To Mary's womb God sent his son. ***(Mary and Joseph walk behind the children gathered behind the clock)***

Accompanying words: *Luke 2: 4* So Joseph went up from the town of Nazareth in Galilee to Judea, to Bethlehem the town of David, because he belonged to the house and line of David. He went there to register with Mary, who was pledged to be married to him and was expecting a child.

Child 1: Dark was the night. ***(wait four beats)*** The sounds were few. ***(wait four beats)*** When suddenly God's power burst through. ***(Mary and Joseph come out in front – Mary carrying baby)*** A child was born for me – for you. ***(Mary places baby in manger. She and Joseph position themselves beneath the clock)*** See our Saviour in the hay.

Child 2: It's the beginning of a brand new day. ***(clock hand moved to twelve o'clock position. Ticking gives way to sound of chiming bells)***

Accompanying words: *Luke 2: 8-14* ... The angel said to them, 'Do not be afraid. I bring you good news of great joy that will be for all people. Today in the town of David a Saviour has been born to you; he is Christ the Lord...'
(everyone sings carol 'Hark, the Herald Angels sing')

APPLICATION

Theme: God works through time and history

Explore: The Messiah

In the Old Testament the prophets Jeremiah, Isaiah, Malachi, Micah and Zechariah all prophesy the coming of a great Messiah or Saviour (Isaiah 9:6-7, Jeremiah 49:5-6, Zechariah 9:9-10). Many Jews believed that the Messiah would be a great military leader but the angel told Joseph that Jesus was to be a different kind of Saviour – one who would 'save his people from their sins' (Matthew 1: 21).

Chat

Imagine God creating a 'to do' list, starting with his call to Abraham, in preparation for the birth of Jesus. Get everyone to think of things that would need to go on the list and write them on 'post-its'. Then draw out a big clock face and stick the 'post-its' round the outside in the right order.

Think

Ask the children to think of things that finally appear after a hidden time of preparation, e.g. a freshly baked cake, a plant shoot above the ground, a butterfly from a chrysalis. Praise God for all the things he did in preparation for the birth of Jesus. How can we prepare to celebrate his birth?

DRAMA 28

THE CHRISTMAS ALPHABET

AGE 6+

SUBJECT: **The Birth of Jesus**

BIBLE READING: **Matthew 2:1-12**

DRAMA NOTES: Suitable for performance at Christmas.

Cast: Two narrators and 2 – 7 children to hang up letters.
Staging: The two narrators stand beside a length of string suspended between two chairs to make a line on which letters may be hung.
Props: Clipboards, seven large sheets of paper folded in half to hang over line: **Sheet 1** hangs with the letter **E** on one side and **O** on the other; **Sheet 2** has **A** on one side and **G** on the other; **Sheet 3** has **H** on one side and **E** on the other; **Sheet 4** has **I** on one side and **A** on the other; **Sheet 5** has **S** on one side and **V** on the other; **Sheet 6** has **S** on one side and **E** on the other; **Sheet 7** has **M** on one side and **L** on the other.

Narrator 1: Ladies and Gentlemen, welcome to the Christmas Alphabet Show – the show where you get to meet the most important letters in the Christmas story.

Narrator 2: And tonight our first letter is ***(consults clipboard)*** the letter one.

Narrator 1: Don't be daft. One is a number. Read the letter after the number.

Narrator 2: Oh sorry! Our first letter is E.

Narrator 1: Bring on the letter E. ***(enter child 1 with letter E facing audience)***

Child 1: This is 'E' for engaged. ***(if you have 7 children carrying on letters, the child stays behind the letter, otherwise the child hangs the letter on the line and goes back offstage)***

Narrator 2: You mean the Christmas story starts with someone not being able to get through on the phone?

Narrator 1: ***(sighs)*** No. It begins with an engagement. Over 2000 years ago, in the town of Nazareth, a carpenter called Joseph was engaged to a girl called Mary.

Narrator 2: Sweet. ***(looks at clipboard)*** The next letter is A. I bet that's A for A-ttractive. Joseph found Mary attractive. ***(enter child 2 with letter A)***

Child 2: This is A for angel. ***(sets letter A to the right of letter E)***

Narrator 2: A for Angel! How come?

Narrator 1: Because God sent an angel to tell Mary she was going to be the mother of his son. And then, when Mary became pregnant, he sent an angel to Joseph in a dream and told him not to be afraid to marry Mary, because the baby she was expecting was very special.

Narrator 2: Which means the next letter is W for wedding, right?

Narrator 1: Wrong. The next letter is the letter H. ***(enter child 3 with letter H)***

Child 3: This is H for Herod. ***(sets letter H to the right of letter)***

Narrator 2: That makes me think of a HUGE department store, with Christmas lights and Santa Claus and loads of expensive presents…

Narrator 1: He/she said Herod – not Harrods. King Herod was king of the land where Mary and Joseph lived. At that time all the Jews had to take part in a big census, which meant everyone had to go to their home towns to register their names.

Narrator 2: ***(studying clipboard while narrator 1 speaks)*** Hey, guess what! The next letter is me.

Narrator 1: No it's not.

Narrator 2: Yes it is. Look. It says so on my list. Letter 4 is I, ***(points to him/herself)*** and I is me.

Narrator 1: I isn't you.

Narrator 2: I know it isn't you. It's me!

Narrator 1: No, I mean… Oh never mind… bring on the next letter. ***(enter child 4 with letter I)***

Child 4: This is 'I' for innkeeper. ***(hangs I between letter E and letter A)***

Narrator 2: But I'm not an innkeeper!

Narrator 1: Exactly. The I in the Christmas story is for an innkeeper who owned an inn in the town of Bethlehem. Mary and Joseph travelled to Bethlehem because that was Joseph's home town. But when they got there the town was so full they couldn't find anywhere to spend the night. This innkeeper allowed them to sleep in a stable beside his inn. And guess what happened that night?

Narrator 2: The inn caught fire?

Narrator 1: Mary had her baby.

Narrator 2: In the middle of the fire!

Narrator 1: There was no fire. Mary had her baby in the middle of the night. She called him Jesus and laid him in a manger. And our next two letters remind us what happened next. ***(enter children 5 & 6, both showing the letter S to the audience)***

Child 5: This is S for shepherd.

Child 6: And this is S for star. ***(they hang the letters between E and I)***

Narrator 2: So what about S for special? I thought you said Mary's baby was special.

Narrator 1: Actually, that's the first sensible thing you've said today. Mary's baby ***was*** special. Jesus was so special that God sent a whole choir of angels to announce the great news of his birth and tell a group of shepherds to go and see him.

Narrator 2: I get it. The shepherds went to see the star who was baby Jesus.

Narrator 1: The shepherds ***did*** go to see baby Jesus, but the star in the Christmas story was a real bright shining star which God set in the sky as another sign of his son's birth... which brings us to our seventh letter... the letter 'M'. ***(enter child 7 with letter M)***

Child 7: This is M for Magi. ***(sets letter M to the left of letter E – the letters should now spell the word MESSIAH)***

Narrator 2: Magic?

Narrator 1: No, Magi. The Magi were wise men who followed the star and finally found baby Jesus and gave him gifts. Now look at the letters of our Christmas alphabet. Can you read what they say?

Narrator 2: MESS – I – AH

Narrator 1: The Messiah is the Saviour sent from God. God sent his son Jesus into the world to save people from all the wrong things they'd done and to show them what he was really like.

Narrator 2: ***(excitedly)*** Wait... wait... I've just noticed something. There are other letters on the back of these letters.

Narrator 1: How do you mean?

Narrator 2: Look... turn the last three letters round... ***(children turn round I A H to show A G E)*** and you've got the word message. The Messiah came to earth with a **message.**

Narrator 1: Hey... that's good.

Narrator 2: It gets better. Take away the last three letters... ***(children remove A G E)*** and what have we got?

Narrator 1: A mess!

Narrator 2: Which is the way the world was before Jesus came. But Jesus, the Messiah, came to earth with a message from God. Now turn the other letters round... ***(children turn round remaining four letters to show L O V E)*** and that message was a message of love.

APPLICATION

Theme: The message of Christmas

Explore: The Christmas Story

The story of the birth of Jesus is told in two books in the Bible, the Gospel of Matthew and the Gospel of Luke. Luke tells how the angel appeared to Mary (Luke 1:26) and Matthew tells how an angel appeared in a dream to Joseph (Matthew 1:20). Luke also tells the story of what happened the night Jesus was born (Luke 2:1–20) while Matthew tells the story of the Magi (Matthew 2:1–12).

Chat

Bring in a selection of Christmas cards and ask the children to pick out the ones that point to the true message of Christmas. Ask them which is their favourite and why.

Think

How does Jesus show us what God is like?

DRAMA 29

FIT FOR LIFE

AGE 8+

SUBJECT: **Jesus and John the Baptist**

BIBLE READING: **John 1:35–40**

DRAMA NOTES: Suitable for group performance.

Cast: Two narrators, John the Baptist, Jesus, 3 + followers/disciples (cast may be reduced by having same person play John the Baptist and third disciple or increased by adding in more followers).
Staging: The drama opens in a fitness studio. 'John the Baptist Fitness Club' sign is propped on a chair. The narrators are side by side, stage right.
Props: Signs saying 'JOHN THE BAPTIST FITNESS CLUB' and 'FIGHT SPIRITUAL FLAB HERE', CD player and CDs of aerobic music and worship songs.

Narrator 1: Many years ago a man called John the Baptist opened a special 'Keep Fit' studio on the banks of the river Jordan. ***(enter John with 'Fight spiritual flab here' sign, which he props up against chair)***

Narrator 2: Lots of people came to John's studio. ***(enter followers)***

Narrator 1: Most looked strong on the outside. ***(followers display muscles)***

Narrator 2: But spiritually they were weak, flabby and out of shape. ***(followers flop forwards)***

Narrator 1: What they needed was a coach. ***(followers move behind John and mime sitting side by side in an imaginary coach with John at the wheel)***

Narrator 2: No, not *that* sort of coach.

Narrator 1: They needed a spiritual fitness coach who could make them fit for eternity. ***(followers move apart, still behind John and mime praying)***

Narrator 2: John knew he couldn't do that. ***(John shakes head and points to heaven)***

Narrator 1: But he believed he'd been sent to prepare the way for the real fitness coach...

Narrator 2: ...by helping people limber up.

Narrator 1: So John led the people in a special 'In, Out – Turn About' limbering up routine. ***(music starts – John and followers mime going down under water and back up – then turning around. They keep this up while narrators speak)***

Narrator 2: This involved them getting baptised in the river Jordan...

Narrator 1: ...and turning away from bad habits.

Narrator 2: In, Out – Turn About. In, Out – Turn About. In, Out – Turn About...

Narrator 1: Then one day John noticed someone joining in the routine who didn't need to limber up because he was already perfectly fit. ***(enter Jesus, who joins in routine)***

Narrator 2: The man's name was Jesus.

Narrator 1: John told his followers that Jesus was the real fitness coach. ***(John points to Jesus)***

Narrator 2: And then he retired. ***(John picks up both signs and exits – music fades)***

Narrator 1: After that, some of John's followers went back to their weak, flabby ways ***(exit optional followers)*** but two men were keen to see what Jesus had to offer. ***(two followers approach Jesus)***

Narrator 2: Jesus invited them to try his fitness programme for a day.

Narrator 1: And they jumped ***(followers leap)*** at the chance.

Narrator 2: Over the next few hours the two men discovered… ***(begin to play worship music softly)*** that being coached by Jesus was completely different from being coached by anyone else. ***(Jesus beckons followers stage left and mimes telling them something)*** Jesus' words were powerful.

Narrator 1: He made them feel totally alive.

Narrator 2: So that night one of them raced off home. ***(exit Andrew stage right, while Jesus and friend sit down and mime sleeping)***

Narrator 1: Next morning he was back with his brother Simon. ***(enter Andrew and Simon. Friend moves centre stage to greet them)***

Narrator 2: Andrew told Simon that he and his friend had discovered the secret of getting fit for eternity.

Narrator 1: Of course Simon thought he knew it already. ***(Simon mimes weight-lifting)***

Narrator 2: But Andrew said the secret wasn't weight-lifting... ***(Andrew and friend shake their heads. Simon mimes press ups)***

Narrator 1: ...or press-ups... ***(Andrew and friend shake their heads. Simon mimes swimming)***

Narrator 2: ...or swimming... ***(Andrew and friend shake their heads. Simon mimes running on spot)***

Narrator 1: ...or running on the spot... ***(Andrew and friend shake their heads. Simon holds stomach)***

Narrator 2: ...or even going on a diet! ***(Andrew and friend shake their heads)***

Narrator 1: It was something completely different.

Narrator 2: Then Andrew introduced Simon to Jesus. ***(Jesus moves towards Simon)***

Narrator 1: And the moment Jesus looked him in the eyes, Simon understood. ***(Jesus takes Simon by the shoulders and looks him in the eyes)***

Narrator 2: He knew immediately that Jesus had superhuman power.

Narrator 1: And people got fit for eternity by trusting their lives to him. ***(Andrew, John and Simon kneel)***

APPLICATION

Theme: Spiritual fitness

Explore: John the Baptist

John the Baptist was God's appointed messenger (predicted in Isaiah 40:3 and Malachi 4:5) to announce the arrival of Jesus. He prepared the way for Jesus' teaching by telling people to turn away from their sin. When he told King Herod his illegal marriage was sinful, he was imprisoned and later killed. While he was in prison, Jesus sent him a special message of encouragement and said that John was the greatest prophet that ever lived (Matthew 11:2–14).

The first disciples

Jesus chose twelve followers to be his special messengers or 'apostles'. Fisherman Andrew was one of the twelve and his brother Simon became the leader of the group. Jesus changed Simon's name to Peter, meaning 'rock'.

Chat

Have a 'keep fit' challenge. Afterwards chat about the differences between someone who is physically fit and someone who isn't. Then ask about spiritual fitness. What are the signs that someone is spiritually fit for eternity? How do you get that way?

Think

Ask children to think of things they can do to keep fit spiritually.

DRAMA 30

DON'T WORRY

AGE 6+

SUBJECT: **Jesus teaches about worry**

BIBLE READING: **Matthew 6:25–34**

DRAMA NOTES: Suitable for reading (possibly using PowerPoint illustrations) or performance.

Cast: Sophie, Chippy, Stephen (should be played by an adult dressed as a schoolboy), narrator, reader (optional – narrator could do this).
Staging: Sleeping bag centre stage, Sophie in large cardboard window box stage left, narrator stage right.
Props: Sleeping bag, football, Bible, box, sound of birdsong (optional).

Narrator: Sophie was a sunflower.
She could nod and sway and bloom.
But Sophie wasn't happy.
Here's the reason for her gloom.
Worry made her droopy
and turned her highs to lows.
She feared she'd lose her petals.
Sophie worried about clothes.

(Sophie nods and sways – ends up with her head down, looking depressed. Enter Chippy stage left)

Narrator: Chippy was a sparrow.
He could hop and chirp and fly.
But Chippy wasn't happy,
and here's the reason why.
Worry stopped him singing
and made poor Chippy brood.
He kept wondering what would happen
if he ran out of food.

(Chippy hops and flaps and ends up beside Sophie looking depressed. Enter Stephen stage left – if played by an adult he crouches to make himself smaller)

Narrator: Stephen was a schoolboy.
He could jump and play and run.
But Stephen wasn't happy -
here's why he had no fun.
Worry gave him nightmares
and spoilt his appetite.
He thought his legs weren't long enough.
Steve worried about his height.

(Stephen plays with football, then sits down on sleeping bag looking miserable)

Narrator: Now Stephen had a Bible.
One night, awake in bed,
he opened up his Bible
and this is what he read.

(Stephen picks up Bible from beside sleeping bag and opens it)

Reader: 'Can worry make you grow taller?
Look how the flowers grow. They don't work hard to make their clothes. But I tell you that Solomon with all his wealth wasn't as well clothed as one of them.
Look at the birds in the sky! They don't plant or harvest...
Yet your Father in heaven takes care of them.
Why do you have such little faith?'

Narrator: As Stephen read these words aloud,
his voice was overheard
by a weary drooping sunflower
and a gloomy songless bird.

(Stephen lies down. Chippy hops towards sleeping bag and Sophie leans towards it)

Narrator: 'Did you hear that?' chirped Chippy.
'How could we be so dim?
God cares for flowers and sparrows.
We should be trusting him.'
'Let's try it out,' said Sophie.
'Let's live a different way.
You sing and I'll lift up my head
and bloom from day to day.'

(Sophie and Chippy stop looking depressed. Stephen sits up and stretches)

Narrator: Steve also took to heart the words
he read in bed that night.
Like the sparrow and the sunflower,
he knew that they were right.
From that time on he ate and trained
and, sure enough, he grew.
Each year his legs got longer,
and his faith kept growing too.

(Stephen stands up and moves behind Chippy and Sophie – holds up Bible)

APPLICATION

Theme: God's answer to worry

Explore: Christ's teaching

In Jesus' day, many people called him 'Rabbi' meaning teacher. Throughout his ministry Jesus taught his disciples and the crowds who came to hear him about the 'Kingdom of God'. One of the things that made Jesus stand out as a teacher was the way he spoke – with an inside knowledge that came from his relationship with God (Matthew 7:29).

The Sermon on the Mount

Worry was one of many subjects which Jesus taught about in a sermon known as the 'Sermon on the Mount'. We can read this sermon in Matthew's Gospel (Matthew 5–7) and it probably covers several days of preaching. It is called the 'Sermon on the Mount' because Jesus was sitting on the steeply rising ground on the western side of the Sea of Galilee when he preached.

Chat

On a large sheet of paper draw a stick figure lying in bed with a worried expression on its face. Round the bed ask the group to write or draw some of the thoughts that could be keeping the figure awake. Do they find that problems are bigger at night? Chat about why it makes sense to hand our worries over to God. Give each child a blank, round sticker and ask them to draw a flower shape on it and (if they can) to write the words 'Trust God' inside the flower. They should then stick the flowers over the worries on their picture.

Think

Remember that no worry or problem is bigger than God.

DRAMA 31

FLAGS AT SEA

AGE 8+

SUBJECT: **Jesus calms the storm**

BIBLE READING: **Mark 4:35–41**

DRAMA NOTES: This simple drama is designed to be performed with coloured flags or ribbons. It is most effective when performed to music.

Cast: 6 children to narrate verses and wave flags. Alternatively, the verses could be narrated by an adult.
Staging: Children sit on seats with their flags furled. One by one they stand up and wave their flag as the appropriate verse is narrated.
Props: Coloured flags or ribbons, Two CD players, CDs of appropriate sailing and storm music.

(sailing music)
Verse 1 ***(blue flag waved gently)***
BLUE was the shade of the sky and the sea
as Jesus set out across Lake Galilee.
With a pull of the ropes and a push of the oar
he and his followers sailed from the shore.
(storm music drowns sailing music)

Verse 2 ***(black flag waved violently up and down)***
BLACK was the colour the water became
as a storm blew up with thunder and rain.
Waves tossed the boat high, then flung it down deep
But Jesus said nothing for he was asleep.

Verse 3 ***(white flag made to tremble)***
WHITE is the colour of weakness and fear.
The disciples were white, and the reason was clear.
'Jesus! Wake up!' came their terrified cry.
'This storm is so bad we're all going to die.'

Verse 4 ***(purple flag waved majestically)***
PURPLE is a shade with a royal ring.
Jesus stood up and he spoke like a king.
He took control. He said 'Peace! Be still!'
Wind and waves instantly bowed to his will.
(storm music stops. Sailing music can be heard again)

Verse 5 ***(red flag lowered in a humble bowing motion)***
RED are the faces of those who are blamed.
The disciples felt safe, but also ashamed.
'Why were you afraid?' Jesus wanted to know.
'How is it your faith takes so long to grow?'

Verse 6 ***(gold flag waved gently)***
GOLD is a treasure. It speaks of the worth
of trusting in Jesus while we live on earth.
And gold was the shade of the sunset that day
as the disciples sailed thankfully into the bay.

APPLICATION

Theme: Testing times

Explore: The Sea of Galilee

The Sea of Galilee is a big freshwater lake thirteen miles long and up to seven miles wide, surrounded by mountains. In Jesus' day it was an important source of food and work for the people who lived in the area and Jesus began his ministry on its shores. The lake was also known as the Lake of Gennesaret and the Sea of Tiberias.

The disciples

Jesus chose twelve men to be his special followers or disciples. They included five fishermen – Simon Peter, Andrew (Peter's brother), James, John (James' brother) and Philip. The other disciples were Bartholomew (also known as Nathanael), Matthew (a tax collector), Thomas, another James, Thaddaeus, Simon the Zealot and Judas Iscariot. Jesus was also supported in his ministry by a group of women who included Mary Magdalene, Joanna and Susanna (Luke 8:2-3).

Chat

Read or retell the story of Jesus calming the storm. (This story is also told as *The Boat Trip* in *50 Five Minute Stories*, published by Children's Ministry). Then have the children sit in a circle. Ask each of them to make a sound representing wind, thunder, lightning, rough sea, etc. (use percussion instruments if they are available). At a given signal, they all make their sounds softly at first but progressing to full blast. As soon as the command 'Peace!' is given all the noise should stop. Then chat about how the noise can be fun… but only because everyone knows it is under control and won't go on forever. Chat about the difference it would have made to the disciples if, when the storm blew up, they had really believed they had the Son of God in the boat with them and that everything was under his control.

Think

God wants to turn our testing times (when things go wrong) into learning times (when we discover more about him).

DRAMA 32

THE MEAN GREEN DRAGON

AGE 8+

SUBJECT: **The Good Samaritan**

BIBLE READING: **Luke 10:30-37**

DRAMA NOTES: Suitable for group reading or performance.

Cast: Two narrators, woodcutter, dragon, two girls, two knights, ambulance driver and assistant (girls, knights, ambulance driver and assistant may be played by the same two actors).
Staging: Empty stool centre stage. Narrators stage left.
Props: Two red hooded cloaks (or anoraks), green hooded cloak (or anorak), stool, cardboard axe, cardboard sword and shield, mobile phone, credit card.

Narrator 1: Jesus told a story which went *something* like this.

Narrator 2: Once upon a time there was a woodcutter… ***(enter woodcutter eagerly waving axe)***

Narrator 1: …who was too old to chop wood. ***(woodcutter sighs and lowers axe)***

Narrator 2: He spent his days sitting on a three-legged stool watching the world go by. ***(woodcutter sits down on stool, looks right and left)***

Narrator 1: One day two young maidens… ***(enter two girls wearing red cloaks with hoods)*** came skipping down the path towards him.

Narrator 2: Sweet!

Narrator 1: No, scary. They were from the Little Red Riding Hood gang. ***(girls pull up hoods)*** Before you could say Humpty Dumpty, they knocked the woodcutter to the ground, broke his three-legged stool, and made off with his axe. ***(girls push woodcutter to the ground, knock over stool and exit with axe)***

Narrator 2: The poor woodcutter passed out with shock. ***(woodcutter tries to get up then falls back to the ground)***

Narrator 1: Not good. An old man like that lying on the ground! He could get hypothermia.

Narrator 2: Before long a noble knight in shining armour came galloping along the path. ***(sound of hoof beats – enter knight)*** The noble knight spotted the woodcutter and got off his horse for a closer look. ***(knight dismounts and looks at woodcutter)***

Knight 1: I say, what have we here?

Narrator 1: He saw that the poor old man was in a bad way. ***(woodcutter groans and shivers)***

Knight 1: This man needs help.

Narrator 2: But the noble knight was trying to catch a mean, green dragon before it reached the village on the other side of the forest.

Narrator 1: So he jumped back onto his horse and off he rode. ***(exit knight)***

Narrator 2: A few minutes passed.

Narrator 1: And along came *another* noble knight in shining armour. ***(enter second knight)***

Narrator 2: This second noble knight also spotted the poor woodcutter and got off his horse for a closer look. ***(knight dismounts and looks at woodcutter)***

Knight 2: I say, what have we here?

Narrator 1: He also saw that the old man was in a bad way. ***(woodcutter groans and shivers)***

Knight 2: This man needs help *urgently*.

Narrator 2: And then…

Narrator 1: …because he too was trying to catch a mean, green dragon before it reached the village on the other side of the forest…

Narrator 2: …this second noble knight jumped back on his horse and rode off.

Narrator 1: By this stage the poor woodcutter didn't know where he was or what was going on. ***(woodcutter sits up)***

Woodcutter: Where am I? What time is it?

Narrator 2: He was lapsing into a coma…***(woodcutter slumps back)***

Narrator 1: ...which was probably a good thing, because next to arrive on the scene was... wait for it.... a *mean, green dragon.* ***(enter dragon who should just be an ordinary person dressed in green)***

Narrator 2: Come off it. That isn't a dragon. In my book dragons breathe fire and have scales and horns and a tail... ***(dragon is kneeling down beside woodcutter, listening to his chest)***

Dragon: Excuse me, but can we just get on with the story. This old man is in a bad way.

Narrator 2: Oh, all right then.

Narrator 1: Even though he knew the woodcutter hated dragons, the mean, green dragon covered the old man with his cloak.... ***(dragon covers woodcutter with cloak)***

Narrator 2: ...and sent for an ambulance. ***(dragon takes out mobile)***

Narrator 1: Then he rang a carpenter and asked him to make the woodcutter a new three-legged stool...

Narrator 2: ...and he paid for it on visa. ***(dragon produces credit card)***

Narrator 1: Moments later the sound of an ambulance siren broke the leafy silence.

Narrator 2: Knowing the woodcutter would be in safe hands, the mean, green dragon escaped to his home on the other side of the forest. ***(exit dragon)***

Narrator 1: The woodcutter was taken to hospital. ***(enter ambulance crew who exit with woodcutter)***

Narrator 2: And they all lived happily ever after.

Narrator 1: Except for one thing.

Narrator 2: Which is?

Narrator 1: Some folk are probably wondering why the mean, green dragon had a mobile and a visa card instead of horns and a tail.

Narrator 2: Well, obviously it's because no-one had time to make a dragon costume.

Narrator 1: Wrong. It's because the mean, green dragon was human. You see, Meangreen was the name of the village on the other side of the forest. The people who lived in the woodcutter's village nicknamed the people of Meangreen 'dragons' because they hated them.

Narrator 2: So the whole point of the story is that the Meangreen dragon was really a human being.

Narrator 1: That's right. He was a big-hearted human being who loved his neighbour.

Narrator 2: Even though his neighbour didn't love him back.

Narrator 1: And *that's* what Jesus tells his followers to do.

APPLICATION

Theme: Loving your neighbour

Explore: Parables

A parable is a story about ordinary things which teaches a spiritual truth. Jesus told the parable of the Good Samaritan to teach people about loving their neighbour. He used parables to teach about many other things including prayer (Luke 11:5-8, Luke 18:1-8), wealth (Luke 12:16-21) and God's love (Matthew 18:12-14).

The Samaritans

The Samaritans lived in Samaria, which lay between the Jewish provinces of Galilee and Judea. Jews didn't want to have any dealings with the Samaritans. They looked down on them and called them dogs because they weren't pure Jews and had different religious practices. But when Jesus was in Samaria he talked with a Samaritan woman, and many Samaritans trusted him. (Luke 9, John 4). (This story is retold in *50 Stories for Special Occasions*, published by Children's Ministry.)

Chat

There's a well-known rhyme, 'Sticks and stones can break my bones, but names will never hurt me.' How is this true? How is it untrue? Chat about what the group think Jesus would say to someone he heard talking about another group or race of people as if they were animals. How does he want us to treat each other?

Think

Ask the children to think of someone who is different from them. How do they treat them? Pray with them that God will help us to really love our neighbours.

DRAMA 33

THE CHEAT

AGE 8+

SUBJECT: **Zacchaeus**

BIBLE READING: **Luke 19:1-10**

DRAMA NOTES: Suitable for group reading or performance.

Cast: Narrator, Zacchaeus, Jesus, crowd of Jews (3+).
Staging: Narrator stands stage left. There is a chair positioned back centre stage.

Narrator: One day a small man called Zacchaeus set out for work, planning to add to his wealth. ***(enter Zacchaeus stage right, rubbing his hands. He takes centre stage)***

Zacchaeus: Matthew owes six talents. But I'll charge him ten talents. That means I'll have four talents for myself.

Narrator: Zacchaeus was the chief tax collector in Jericho. He worked for the Romans. He had become rich by making people pay too much tax and keeping the extra money. ***(enter crowd stage right)*** The other Jews in Jericho hated Romans.

Crowd: ***(shaking fists and booing)*** We hate Romans.

Narrator: They hated paying taxes.

Crowd: ***(shaking fists and booing)*** We hate taxes.

Narrator: And they couldn't stand Zacchaeus.

Crowd ***(pointing and booing)***

Jew 1: Ugh! Zacchaeus.

Jew 2: He doesn't deserve to be called a Jew.

Jew 3: ***(self-righteously)*** He's a cheat and a traitor and God will punish him for his sins.

Narrator: That day Zacchaeus discovered that Jesus of Nazareth, the famous miracle-worker, had come to town. There was a big crowd of people trying to see him.

Crowd: ***(moves centre stage in front of Zacchaeus)*** Jesus! Jesus! Jesus!

Narrator: Zacchaeus wanted to see Jesus too. But he was so small, he couldn't see anything from the back of the crowd.

Zacchaeus: I know, I'll try jumping. Maybe I can jump high enough to see Jesus. Here goes...***(jumps)***

Jew 1: Ouch! Cut that out, Creep. That was my toe you landed on.

Zacchaeus: ***(falsely)*** Sor-ry. I know, I'll try pushing. Maybe I can push hard enough to see Jesus. Here goes... ***(jostles and pushes)***

Jew 2: Hey, quit pushing, Shrimp. Keep your elbows to yourself.

Zacchaeus: Sor-ry. I know, I'll try crawling. Maybe I can crawl in far enough to get a look at Jesus' feet. Here goes... ***(drops to the floor and tries to crawl between legs)***

Jew 3: Zacchaeus, if you don't get your sneaky tax collector's head out from between my legs this minute, I'll happily trample you to death.

Zacchaeus: Sor-ry. I know, maybe I could just...

Jews: 1, 2 & 3: GET LOST!

Zacchaeus: Oh well, if that's how you feel...

Jews: 1, 2 & 3: CLEAR OFF!

Zacchaeus: You'll pay for this when you get your next tax bill. ***(moves stage right and crouches with his head in his hands)***

Narrator: Zacchaeus couldn't get through the crowd. But he still wanted to see Jesus. Suddenly he had a brainwave. ***(Zacchaeus stands up)***

Zacchaeus: Zacchaeus, you're a genius!

Narrator: His idea was to run on ahead of everyone else and pull himself up into the leafy branches of a tall shady sycamore tree. ***(crowd exit stage right, Zacchaeus runs centre stage – stands on chair)***

Zacchaeus: That's it! A first class view and it isn't costing me a penny.

Narrator: Sure enough, a few minutes later, the crowd came thronging down the road towards the tree. ***(enter cheering crowd – who position themselves between the chair and stage right)***

Crowd: ***(cheering)*** Jesus! Jesus! Jesus!

Narrator: At long last Zacchaeus saw Jesus. ***(enter Jesus stage right)*** He seemed to be in a hurry. Everywhere people were shouting out to get his attention.

Jew 1: Jesus, please bless me.

Jew 2: Lord, I need a miracle.

Jew 3: Master, I've got an important question…

(Jesus walks past crowd straight to 'the tree' and looks up)

Jesus: Hey, Zacchaeus. Come down, would you. Let's go round to your place.

Zacchaeus: To my place! Oh yes, please. I'd be honoured. ***(jumps down)***

Narrator: Almost fainting with shock, Zacchaeus walked along the street with Jesus. ***(Zacchaeus and Jesus walk off together and exit stage left)*** The crowd could hardly believe it.

Jew 1: Jesus has gone off for tea with Zacchaeus.

Jew 2: With Zacchaeus – you mean with that little rat of a tax collector!

Jew 3: Jesus ought to know better than to eat with a man like him. ***(crowd exit stage right)***

Narrator: But Zacchaeus was exactly the sort of man Jesus wanted to eat with. For when Jesus looked at Zacchaeus, he didn't see a rat. ***(enter Jesus and Zacchaeus. Jesus sits on the chair centre stage, with Zacchaeus at his feet)*** He saw someone longing for forgiveness. Someone who really wanted to be different. And that day, thanks to Jesus, Zacchaeus did become different.

First he cried a little. Then he smiled a lot. Next thing he was making an important announcement. ***(enter crowd, who stand left of centre)***

Zacchaeus: ***(standing up – and shouting)*** Here and now I'm giving half of what I own to the poor. And anyone I've cheated will get back four times what I took. ***(moves over and gives some money to Jew 2)***

Narrator: Jesus made an announcement too.

Jesus: From now on Zacchaeus is a true child of God. ***(goes and stands with an arm around Zacchaeus, in the middle of the crowd)***

Narrator: So our story ends with some very puzzled people.

Jew 1: Something's happened to Zacchaeus. He's giving money away!

Narrator: And with some very delighted people.

Jew 2: Hey, guess what. I've got back far more tax than I paid!

Narrator: And with one very happy Zacchaeus.

Zaccheus: This is brilliant. I'm clean inside. Making friends with Jesus has changed my life.

APPLICATION

Theme: Putting things right

Explore: Tax Collectors

In Jesus' day, Jews who acted as tax collectors were hated and despised. This was mainly because the money they collected was passed on to their Roman masters and used to support a system where people worshipped pagan gods. It was also because tax collectors, like Zacchaeus, often demanded more money than they should and kept the extra for themselves.

Chat

Look at a couple of news items in magazines or newspapers, where people have done something wrong that has had a bad effect on someone else. Discuss what that person could do to put things right. Chat about how it feels to put things right with others. Then talk about what it means, and how it feels, to put things right with God.

Think

Ask the children to imagine that Jesus calls at their homes? What do they do? What do they show him? What do they talk about?

DRAMA 34

I'M RICH

AGE 10+

SUBJECT: **The Rich Young Man**

BIBLE READING: **Mark 10:17-22**

DRAMA NOTES: Suitable for group reading or performance.

Cast: Two narrators, Fred, beggar.
Staging: Narrators side by side stage right. Fred centre stage.
Props: *(all optional)* Low archway/entrance (could be made out of cardboard boxes) with sign saying 'New Life' above it, T-shirt, trainers, monkey-nut, wallet.

Narrator 1: Once upon a time there was a young man.

Fred: ***(waving)*** Hi! I'm Rich.

Narrator 1: His name was Fred.

Narrator 2: But he said his name was Rich.

Narrator 1: No he didn't.

Narrator 2: Yes he did. He said, 'Hi, I'm Rich.'

Narrator 1: Well what he really meant to say was 'Hi, I'm Fred and I'm rich.'

Fred: Hi, I'm Fred and I'm *very* rich.

Narrator 2: Ah, that explains the diamond-studded trainers. ***(Fred lifts his feet)***

Narrator 1: And the monkey-nut sized mobile. ***(Fred pretends to take monkey-nut out of his ear, holds it on his open palm and puts it back in his ear again)***

Narrator 2: And the gold embossed designer T-shirt.

Fred: ***(takes out wallet and hands narrator 2 a note)*** Here – take this and get yourself one. It can be your birthday present.

Narrator 2: Wow! Thanks, Rich… I mean Fred.

Narrator 1: This sort of generous action was typical of the young man. He might have been very rich, but he was an all round decent guy. He helped his maid load the dishwasher. He fed stray dogs. And he bought all his friends *huge* presents on their birthdays. ***(chorus off stage – 'Wow! Thanks, Fred')***

Narrator 2: I bet he had loads of friends.

Fred: ***(nodding)*** With loads of birthdays.

Narrator 1: But even though Fred got a million text messages every day, there were times when he felt lonely.

Narrator 2: What! With all those friends!

Narrator 1: He used to ask himself…

Fred: ***(nodding and sighing)*** Does anyone know the *real* me?

Narrator 1: ***(Fred mimes while narrator speaks)*** And even though he and his friends went skiing and white-water rafting and rock-climbing and scuba-diving, he always felt restless. He used to ask himself…

Fred: Is this all there is?

Narrator 1: On holiday he would stand at the top of a ski slope covered in sparkling white snow and think…

Fred: I'm a mess.

Narrator 2: Come off it, Fred. Your trainers and T-shirt are spotless!

Fred: I mean I'm a mess inside.

Narrator 2: I'd never have guessed.

Fred: Most people don't.

Narrator 1: One night Fred went to bed. ***(Fred lies down)*** While he slept, he had a dream and in his dream he met a beggar. ***(enter beggar who taps Fred awake)***

Narrator 1: The moment the beggar looked at him, Fred realised this guy knew him through and through.

Fred: You can tell what I'm thinking, can't you? ***(beggar nods)***

Narrator 2: Awesome!

Narrator 1: Next thing, Fred was blurting out the questions no-one else even knew he was asking.

Fred: Tell me how can I get clean inside and be sure of heaven?

Narrator 1: At this the beggar led Fred to a small doorway. ***(beggar leads Fred to entrance)*** There was a sign above the entrance. It said 'New Life'. Next thing, the beggar was on the other side of the doorway, beckoning Fred through.

Narrator 2: It's a very low door.

Narrator 1: That wasn't a problem. Fred dropped to his knees. He really wanted to go through.... but he couldn't...

Narrator 2: Why not?

Narrator 1: It was as if there was an invisible barrier across the doorway. ***(Fred struggles against invisible barrier)*** Fred called to the beggar.

Fred: Tell me how to get through.

Narrator 1: Immediately the beggar told him... ***(beggar holds out hands as if hanging from a cross)***

Beggar: ...empty your pockets. Leave everything you own outside the door.

Narrator 2: What! You mean the beggar expected Fred to leave his mobile and his wallet and go through the door without them.

Narrator 1: The beggar was offering him the adventure of a lifetime.

Narrator 2: Well, what are you waiting for? Go for it, Fred.

Fred: But I'm rich. My friends all expect me to buy things. I can't face them empty-handed.

Beggar: I'll be the best friend you'll ever have.

Narrator 2: You heard the man, Fred. Fred, what are you doing? ***(Fred sits down with his back to doorway)*** He's not going through. Look! He's turned his back on the doorway.

Narrator 1: Fred wanted to follow the beggar but something was stopping him.

Narrator 2: ***(shaking head)*** It's his money. He can't bear to part with it.

Narrator 1: And the question is, if you were very rich, could you?

APPLICATION

Theme: Love of money

Explore: The rich young man

The story of Jesus meeting the rich young man is told in Mark's Gospel. The young man was a good Jew. He knew God's Laws and tried to keep them. Still he wasn't sure where he stood spiritually. His question to Jesus shows that he was worried about what would happen when he died (Mark 10: 7). Jesus' answer helped the young man to see the real problem. His wealth meant more to him than God.

Jesus and money

Jesus was born into a poor family. During the three years when he went about teaching and preaching he had no home (Matthew 8:20). He relied on other people to give him what he needed (Luke 8:3). At the same time, he did not tell everyone who trusted him to leave their homes and possessions (John 12:1-2). The important thing was their willingness to put God first.

Chat

What are the good things about having money? What are the bad things about not having money? Are there any good things about not having money? Eternal life is one very good thing that money can't buy – how do you get it?

Think

Ask the children to imagine they meet Jesus in the street. He invites them into a nearby park and they sit down for a chat. Jesus wants to know about things that are important to them. What do they say?

DRAMA 35

BLIND BART

AGE 6+

SUBJECT: **Jesus heals a blind beggar**

BIBLE READING: **Mark 10:46–52**

DRAMA NOTES: Suitable for reading or performance.

Cast: Narrator, Bartimaeus, friend, Jesus.
Staging: *(optional)* Narrator in front of a sheet. Bartimaeus, Friend and Jesus mime their parts behind the sheet as a shadow play. Sheet is pulled away when Bartimaeus receives his sight. Drama opens with the narrator in the spotlight, stage right.

(enter Bartimaeus led by friend)

Narrator: Blind Bartimaeus had no sight,
His world was always dark as night.
(Bartimaeus sits down and holds up his hands to beg)
Because he couldn't work for pay
he had to beg for food each day.

One morning, seated in the street
Bart heard the distant sound of feet.
(narrator asks audience walk on spot quietly)
'Jesus is coming,' Bart's friend said.
'He has power to raise the dead.'

The footsteps now were getting loud –
(audience walk on the spot more vigorously)
the footsteps of a mighty crowd
of fat folk, thin folk,
(narrator indicates size and shape of people)
follow-with-a grin folk,
strong folk, weak folk,
elegantly sleek folk.

Bartimaeus breathed in deep.
He felt his heart within him leap.
(Bartimaeus crouches)
Where Jesus was he could not tell.
The one thing he could do was yell.
(Bartimaeus puts hands to his mouth)
'Jesus! Saviour! Please help me!'
'Be quiet!' the crowd hissed furiously.
(friend puts restraining hand on his shoulder)
Still Bart kept yelling out his plea.
'Jesus! Saviour! Please help me!'

Then someone shouted, 'Step this way.
Cheer up, Bart. It's your lucky day.
Jesus wants to speak to you.'
(enter Jesus)

All at once Bart left his seat
(Bart stands up and is led to Jesus)
and threw himself at Jesus' feet.
(Bart kneels)
Bart felt a hand upon his head.
(Jesus places his hand on Bart's head)
'I heard you calling,' Jesus said.
'What is it you want me to do?'
And in the instant blind Bart knew
that, as he asked, so it would be.
'Lord,' he cried. 'I want to see.'

'Stand up,' said Jesus. 'You're all right.'
(Bart stands)
Immediately Bart's world grew bright.
(narrator pulls down sheet)
Fingers, faces, elbows, knees,
(Bartimaeus looks friend over)
Flowers, butterflies and bees –
(Bartimaeus looks round)
he saw them all. His eyes had cleared.
'Praise the Lord! I'm healed!' he cheered.

'Faith made you whole, Bart,' Jesus smiled.
(Jesus puts his arm round Bartimaeus)
'Now go and live as God's true child.'

APPLICATION

Theme: God's help

Explore: Beggars

In Jesus' day most people earned their living by doing physical work. This meant that disabled people had to beg on the streets. God's law commanded the Jews to give to those in need (Leviticus 25:35-38) but their lives were still very hard. Another problem for the blind beggar would have been the belief that blindness was a punishment for sin. In John's Gospel there is another story of Jesus healing a blind man in which Jesus makes it very clear that sin had nothing to do with the man's problem (John 9:1-3).

Chat

Talk about some situations where people shout out for help and are rescued. Act them out. The blind beggar was trapped in his blindness. Chat about why he shouted out to Jesus. (Because he believed that Jesus was the Messiah – 'the Son of David' – and would be able to help him.)

Think

Imagine Bartimaeus is making a 'thank you' card for Jesus. What picture might he draw on the front? What words might he write inside? Remember, just as Jesus heard Bartimaeus shouting and stopped to help, so he hears us when we pray and will help us too.

DRAMA 36

FOOTBALL ISLAND

AGE 11+

SUBJECT: **Jesus and the Pharisees**

BIBLE READING: **Matthew 23:1–7**

DRAMA NOTES: A humorous drama, suitable for group reading or performance.

Cast: Narrator, 3 islanders/referees.
Staging: Narrator stage left. Box centre stage. Table with phone to the side.
Props: Plastic box with book inside, football referees' kits, telephone, table.

Narrator 1: Football Island was a small desert island in the middle of nowhere. The islanders who lived there knew nothing of the outside world. ***(enter islanders. They should have coats or dressing gowns over their referee kits)*** One day three islanders found a box on the beach.

Islander 1: ***(picks up box and shakes it)*** It must have been washed up by the tide.

Islander 2: There's something inside. Go on! Open it.

Islander 1: It's a book. ***(reads title)*** 'The Laws of Football.'

Islander 3: Brothers, we've just found the Official Laws of this island.

Islander 2: Sent by the island's owner.

Islander 1: ***(importantly)*** Well, you know what this means?

Islanders 2 & 3: What?

Islander 1: It means we must tell all the islanders about the Laws in this book and make sure they obey them. We'll be the owner's deputies.

Islander 2: Wow! We'll be important.

Islander 3: We'll be *very* important.

Islander 1: We'll be very important *indeed.* ***(exit islanders)***

Narrator: And so the three islanders became experts in the Laws of Football. To make sure everyone knew how important they were, they wore special robes. ***(enter islanders dressed as football referees)*** They even became known by a special name.

Islanders: We're the Referees.

Narrator: And they went around chanting their favourite laws.

Islander 1: A Referee enforces the laws of the game.

Islander 2: A Referee punishes serious offences.

Islander 3: The decisions of a Referee are final.

Narrator: Now the islanders were simple people and soon the Referees had them under their thumbs. They appointed assistants and sent them all over the island with red and yellow cards. ***(islanders pull table centre stage and stand in a line behind it – telephone rings)***

Islander 2: Fine Payment Centre… Your name please? Yes, Farmer Brown, how can we help? One of our assistants has just given you a yellow card for sowing seed in the field you've just bought. What shape is the field? A square! Oh dear, that's bad.

Islander 3: That's *very* bad.

Islander 1: That's very bad *indeed.* ***(chanting)*** The Law says the field of play must be rectangular and at least 90 metres long and 45 metres wide.

Islander 2: So you see, Farmer Brown, you have committed an offence. Yes, I know the Law talks about a 'Field of Play', but those words cover any kind of activity in any kind of field. I'm afraid I'll have to hand you over to our Penalty Department. ***(hands phone to Islander 3)***

Islander 3: Hello, Penalty Department. The fine for a yellow card is three hundred pounds. Just drop the money round to us here at the Payment Centre. Goodbye. ***(puts down phone)***

Islander 2: Three hundred pounds. That's good!

Islander 3: That's *very* good.

Islander 1: That's very… ***(telephone rings)***

Islander 2: Fine Payment Centre. Your name please? Yes, Madam, how can we help? Your daughter got a red card at her wedding and she doesn't know why. Well, what was she wearing at the time?... A long white dress and a veil. Oh dear, that's bad.

Islander 3: That's *very* bad.

Islander 1: That's very bad *indeed.* ***(chanting)*** The Law says all players must wear jerseys or shirts, shorts, thick socks, shinguards and boots.

Islander 2: The white dress, Madame, was your daughter's first offence. And tell me, how many bridesmaids did she have? Two! Well, there you are then – that's her second offence. We all know Law Three, don't we?

Islander 1: A match is made by two teams, each consisting of not more than eleven players. A match may not happen if either team consists of fewer than seven players.

Islander 2: Clearly your daughter should have had at least six bridesmaids on her team. So she had the wrong dress and the wrong number of players. I'm putting you through to our Penalty Department. ***(hands phone to Islander 3)***

Islander 3: Hello! If your daughter doesn't want to be sent off the island, she must pay a five hundred pound fine. Tell her to drop the money round to us here at the Payment Centre. Goodbye. ***(referees rub their hands)***

Narrator: Then one day the phone went silent. The Referees couldn't understand it. They sat in their office for 45 minutes looking in one direction. ***(referees face right)*** And for 45 minutes looking in the other direction. ***(referees face left)*** They even allowed themselves extra time. ***(referees look at watches)*** But the phone didn't ring once. In the end they telephoned an assistant.

Islander 1: ***(dials number)*** Hello there. How come you haven't been fining anyone? Oh, I see. ***(to other referees)*** They've all gone down to the beach.

Islander 2: So? Tell her to fine anyone on the beach without a ticket.

Islander 1: ***(speaks into phone)*** We want you to fine anyone who's... what's that? Sonny won't let you. Who, in the name of football, is Sonny? He's... no, I don't believe it. ***(to other referees)*** She says the owner's son has showed up.

Islander 2: The owner's son!

Islander 3: He must have come to the island to check up on us.

Islander 1: ***(talking to assistant)*** I'm sure he's impressed with the good job we've been doing. What! He *isn't* impressed? ***(to other referees)*** The owner's son doesn't think we're doing a good job. He says we're… oh, the cheek of it!

Islanders 2 & 3: What did he say?

Islander 1: He says we're *robbing* people. He says the Laws of Football are meant to help them play a GAME.

Islander 3: Rubbish! Give me that phone. ***(snatches phone)*** This is the Fine Centre. That jumped up Sonny person… I want you to put me onto him right away… Too busy! Doing what? *Refereeing* a *match*! How dare he! ***(slams phone down)*** Come on, brothers, if the so-called owner's son isn't prepared to keep the Laws of Football, we'll make him sorry. ***(gets up and leads others off stage)***

Islander 2: We'll make him *very* sorry.

Islander 1: We'll make him very sorry *indeed.*

APPLICATION

Theme: Missing the point

Explore: The Pharisees

The Pharisees were a strict religious sect who kept closely to God's Law and added lots of extra rules to make sure people did not break it. There were around 6,000 Pharisees at the time of Jesus, and most were opposed to his teaching. Each Pharisee wore a box called a phylactery on his forehead, containing four pieces of parchment with words from Scripture. Another phylactery, containing one piece of parchment, was strapped to the left arm.

Jesus and the Pharisees

Jesus hated the way the Pharisees made huge demands of ordinary people, turning the Law into a long list of do's and don'ts which only religious experts could keep. Jesus taught that all the commandments could be summed up in the two great commandments – to love God and your neighbour (Matthew 22:34-40). He accused the Pharisees of caring too much about appearances and not enough about what went on in people's hearts.

Chat

Chat about how the young people think this drama connects with the Bible reading. Aim to bring out the fact the Laws of Football were written to help people play a game but the Referees missed the whole point and used the Laws to line their own pockets. In the same way the Old Testament laws were given to guide people in their relationships with God and others. The Pharisees missed the point and used the laws to make themselves look good. Chat about how people can miss the point of what the church is about today.

Think

Jesus got angry with the Pharisees because, although they knew the Laws and kept them outwardly, there was no love in their hearts. Ask God to fill our hearts with love for him and for others.

DRAMA 37

RIDE ON

AGE 6+

SUBJECT: Jesus rides into Jerusalem

BIBLE READING: Luke 19:28-40

DRAMA NOTES: This is a simple rhythmic drama. It can be performed by a drama team up front, or by dividing a large group into four smaller groups. (Ideally, if this is done, it is good to have four folk who are familiar with the drama giving a lead to each of the small groups.)

Cast: Narrator, donkey, Praise leader, Pharisee, heart beat.
Staging: Narrator stage left, voices in a line stage right.
Props: Castanets or similar to make sound of hoof beats, drum, green streamers or ribbons to represent palm branches.

(sound of hoof beats)

Narrator: Clippity clop, clippity clop -
The donkey's hooves made everyone stop.
What excitement! What a thrill!
Jesus was riding up the hill.

Voice 1: *(moving from foot to foot)*
Clippity clop! Clippity clop!
The donkey's hooves went clippety clop.

Narrator: The people hoped Jesus would take up the throne.
They longed to have a King of their own.
They shouted their praise to God on high.
'Hallelujah!' hear them cry.

Voice 2: *(waves streamer)*
'Praise to God! Praise to God!'
The people shouted, 'Praise to God!'

Voice 1: *(moving from foot to foot)*
Clippity clop, clippity clop.
The donkey's hooves went clippity clop.

Narrator: But some of the Pharisees in the crowd
had got together and secretly vowed
to make Jesus sorry for things he had said.
Fearing his power, they wanted him dead.

Voice 3: *(shaking finger)*
'Keep your followers quiet! Keep your followers quiet!'
the Pharisees cried, 'Keep your followers quiet!'

Voice 2: *(waving streamers)*
'Praise to God! Praise to God!'
The people shouted, 'Praise to God!'

Voice 1: ***(moving from foot to foot)***
Clippity clop, clippity clop.
The donkey's hooves went clippety clop.

Narrator: Ahead of Jesus lay sorrow and pain.
But he didn't hold back. He didn't refrain
from doing the will of his Father above.
He simply rode on with a heart full of love.

Voice 4: ***(beating drum to represent heart beat)***
A heart full of love, a heart full of love.
Jesus rode on with a heart full of love.

Voice 4 ***repeats own lines in unison with Voice 3:***
'Keep your followers quiet! Keep your followers quiet!'
the Pharisees cried, 'Keep your followers quiet!'

Voices 3 & 4 ***repeat own lines in unison with Voice 2:***
'Praise to God! Praise to God!'
The people shouted, 'Praise to God!'

Voices 2, 3 & 4 ***repeat own lines in unison with Voice 1:***
Clippity clop, clippity clop.
The donkey's hooves went clippity clop.

Voices 1, 2, 3 & 4 ***all repeat their own lines.***
(Voices 2, 3 & 4 fall silent, but voice 4 continues to beat drum)

Voice 1: Clippity clop, clippity clop Jesus rode on and he didn't stop.
(drum gives three solo double beats before stopping)

APPLICATION

Theme: Determination to do God's will

Explore: Jerusalem

Jerusalem was a very important city for the Jewish people. In Jesus' day the population of the city was around 60,000. Many more people would have been there for the Feast of Passover – a special religious celebration held once a year. Jesus rode into Jerusalem on the Sunday before Passover, knowing he would soon lay down his life in the final act of salvation.

The donkey

The prophet Zechariah prophesied that the Messiah would come riding on a donkey (Zechariah 9:9-10). When Jesus rode into Jerusalem on a donkey, the crowds saw him as a new king, coming to free them from the Romans. They did not understand what he had really come to do.

Chat

Talk about times when children have been determined to do something hard e.g. tying laces, learning to swim, making it to the top of a mountain. What does it feel like to be determined? What difference does it make to the way you act? Then chat about Jesus riding into Jerusalem, even though he knew there were plots to kill him. What made him act the way he did?

Think

How determined are we to do what God wants?

DRAMA 38

TRANSFORMATION SCENE

AGE 11+

SUBJECT: The Resurrection

BIBLE READING: John 20:1-18

DRAMA NOTES: This drama may be performed as a dramatic reading for three voices (substitute Voice Three for chorus) or acted out by a larger group. Throughout the drama, Chorus/Voice Three repeat the same sentence emphasising whichever word is printed in bold.

Cast: (for group performance) Voice One, Voice Two, Mary, Chorus (3+).
Staging: Voices One and Two stage left, Mary and Chorus stage right.

Voice One: Knowing that he would soon be put to death
Jesus tried to prepare his followers for what lay ahead.

Chorus: Jesus said, 'Your sadness will be turned to joy'.

Voice Two: Jesus knew his enemies would be glad when he died.
But his disciples would be heart-broken
and so would all the other folk who believed in him;
people he'd helped; like Mary Magdalene,
(Mary steps forward)
who had followed him ever since he'd healed her.

Chorus: Jesus said, 'Your **sadness** will be turned to joy'.

Voice One: Sadness is a lump we can't swallow,
(Chorus touch their throats)
an emptiness we can't fill,
(Chorus hold their stomachs)
a weight we carry all the time.
(Chorus bend as if weighed down)
Sadness makes us cry. ***(Chorus touch eyes)***

Voice Two: When Jesus was crucified Mary cried. ***(Mary covers her face)***
She cried as she saw his body wrapped in strips of linen
and placed in a tomb. Mary loved Jesus.
(Mary shakes head)
She couldn't imagine life without him.
She couldn't understand why such a terrible thing had happened
to this wonderful man.
(Mary makes bewildered gesture and sinks to ground)

Chorus: Jesus said, 'Your sadness will be **turned** to joy'.

Voice Two: Turning means a change of direction.
It also means one thing becoming something else.

Voice One: On the morning of the third day
(Mary stands up, mimes looking into tomb)
Mary went to the tomb and found it empty.

When she saw the empty tomb she turned
(Mary runs to Chorus)
and ran to fetch two other disciples.
'They have stolen Jesus' body,' she cried.
(Mary talking to Chorus)
Then she turned and ran back to the tomb again.
(Mary runs centre stage)

Voice Two: As Mary wept beside the tomb someone came and spoke to her.
And the moment he said her name
Mary knew ***(Mary clasps hands with joy)***
it was her Lord. Jesus. Alive!

Chorus: Jesus said, 'Your sadness will be turned to **joy**'.

Voice One: Joy makes us jump and shout and laugh through tears.
(Mary runs to Chorus and hugs them)
It makes us want to hug people we wouldn't normally hug,
and makes people we wouldn't normally hug, hug us back.
Joy is infectious. It's like swallowing sunshine -
floating, discovering a patch of heaven on earth.
(Mary joins Chorus)

Chorus: Jesus said, 'Your sadness **will** be turned to joy'.

Voice One: Not *might* be turned;

Voice Two: not *could* be turned;

Voice One: not possibly;

Voice Two: not maybe;

Voice One: not 'if I come out of this OK',

Voice Two: but rather – as surely night becomes day –

Chorus: Jesus said, 'Your **sadness will** be **turned** to **joy**'.

APPLICATION

Theme: What the resurrection means

Explore: Mary Magdalene

The Bible tells us that Mary Magdalene was possessed by seven demons (Mark 16:9). Jesus cast them out and healed her (Luke 8:1-3). After that Mary became part of a band of women who supported Jesus in lots of practical ways. She was the first person Jesus appeared to when he rose from the dead and he gave her the job of telling the other disciples that he was alive (John 20:17). (Mary's story is retold in *50 Five Minute Stories* and in *50 Life-building Stories,* both published by Children's Ministry.)

The Resurrection

Jesus was crucified on Friday, the day before the Jewish Sabbath, and rose from the dead on Sunday, the first day of the week. The Messiah's resurrection was predicted in the Old Testament (Psalm 16:10). Knowing this, the religious leaders persuaded Pilate, the Roman Governor, to place guards outside the tomb in case the disciples tried to steal the body.

Chat

Read the Bible passage with the group. Then ask one of the children to imagine she is Mary. The rest of the group are disciples. Encourage them to act out the scene where Mary tells the disciples about her meeting with Jesus. Go on to chat about some of the things the resurrection of Jesus means for us today e.g. love is stronger than hate, physical death is not the end, Jesus can fill our lives with his resurrection power.

Think

Ask the children to think of people that they know who are sad because someone they love has died. Pray that God will comfort them.

DRAMA 39

WHAT NEXT?

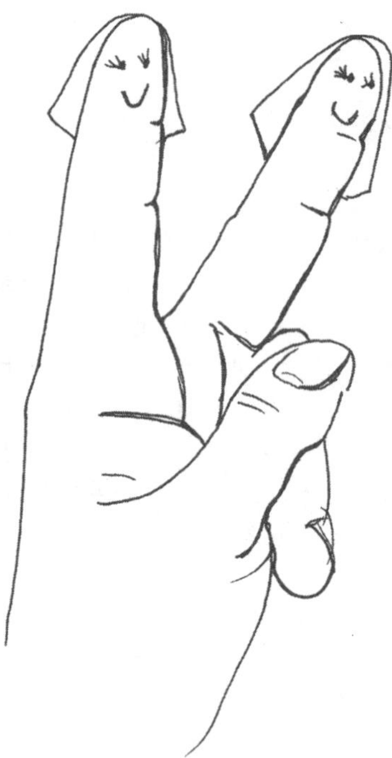

AGE 7+

SUBJECT: The Great Commission

BIBLE READING: Matthew 28:16-20

DRAMA NOTES: This drama is designed to involve any number of children, using their fingers and working in small groups of four. **Child A** in each group uses **two index fingers** to play the parts of **Mary Magdalene** and the **other Mary**. **Child B** uses fingers on **right hand** to play the parts of **five soldiers. Child C** uses fingers on **left hand** to represent **Chief Priests** and fingers of **right hand** to represent the **disciples. Child D** uses **left thumb** as the **angel of the Lord** and **right index finger (or a torch)** to play the part of **Jesus**. Every time a movement word is used (walking, marching, running etc) the group referred to do it on the spot. Go through the drama twice. The first time it should be taken slowly with children copying the actions of four performers who already know what to do and without breaking up to run about at the end. The second time it should be performed fast.
Optional props: Finger puppets, a torch for each group of four.

Narrator: On the first day of the week, after Jesus had been crucified and buried, Mary Magdalene and another Mary ***(Child A holds up 2 fingers)*** set off to **walk** ***(Child A walks on spot)*** to the tomb. Suddenly there was a huge earthquake. The angel of the Lord ***(Child D holds up left thumb)*** appeared at the tomb, rolled back the stone and sat on it. The soldiers who were guarding the tomb ***(Child B holds up right hand)*** trembled ***(Child B fingers quiver)*** and then fainted ***(Child B wrist flops)*** with shock. The angel showed the two women that the tomb was empty ***(Child A and Child D move their hands together)*** and said, 'Go and tell the disciples that Jesus has risen from the dead and is waiting for them in Galilee.' So the women **ran** ***(Child A runs on spot)*** off to pass on this message.

Meanwhile the soldiers woke up. ***(Child B holds up right hand)*** They **ran** ***(Child B runs on spot)*** back into the city to tell the chief priests ***(Child C holds up left hand)*** what had happened. ***(Child B and Child C bring their hands together)*** The last thing the chief priests ***(Child C wiggles fingers)*** wanted, was for people to start believing Jesus had risen from the dead. ***(Child C clenches fist)*** They said to the soldiers, 'Tell everyone that Jesus' disciples stole his body.' ***(Child C and Child B shake hands)*** They gave the soldiers a lot of money and the soldiers **marched** ***(Child B marches on spot)*** away to spread their lies.

Of course, by now, the women ***(Child A holds up two fingers)*** had told the disciples ***(Child C holds up right hand)*** the true story. ***(Child A and C bring hands together)*** As soon as the disciples got Jesus' message they **ran** ***(Child C runs on spot)*** to the mountain in Galilee where he had told them to go. There, Jesus ***(Child D holds up right index finger or turns on torch)*** met them. Jesus gave the disciples a special job. ***(Child D shines torch, or touches finger, on Child C's hand)*** He said, 'People everywhere need to know that I'm alive. So go and make disciples all over the world.' Then, after promising the disciples that his Spirit would always be with them, Jesus went back to heaven. ***(Child D raises finger or torch. Child C waves)*** The disciples watched until he'd vanished out of sight ***(Child D switches off torch or lowers finger)*** Then off they went to share the wonderful news. ***(Children all move around telling each other 'Jesus is alive')***

APPLICATION

Theme: Following instructions

Explore: The Ascension

Forty days after Jesus rose from the dead he went back to heaven. During those forty days Jesus appeared to the disciples at different times. For some, such as Thomas and Peter, he had a special message of encouragement (John 10:24-29, John 21:15-19).
The special instruction written down in Matthew 28:20 is known as 'the Great Commission'.

Chat

Play a Chinese whisper 'instruction' game. Divide children into two teams. Leaders are given an instruction to be whispered from member to member and carried out at the end (e.g. shake hands with x and then sit down and fold your arms). See which team carries out the instruction most accurately in the shortest time. Then chat about Jesus' final instruction to his disciples, bringing out the fact that Jesus promised that, even though they couldn't physically see him any more, he would always be with them.

Think

Ask the children to think of some places they go regularly and write them on inflated balloons. They then knock the balloons to one another. Each time someone catches a balloon they call out the name of the place that is written on it, as they hit it on to someone else. Finish by thanking Jesus that he is with us wherever we are.

PART FOUR

JOIN THE COMPANY

(And Change the World)

DRAMA 40

DR FIXIT

AGE 8+

SUBJECT: **The Holy Spirit**

BIBLE READING: **Acts 2:1–4**

DRAMA NOTES: Suitable for group reading or performance.

Cast: Dr Fixit, Penny Piggybank, Sam Smoke-alarm, Miles Motorbike, All Saints Church, receptionist.
Staging: The scene is a consulting room. Dr Fixit is seated at his/her desk.
Costumes: Characters playing objects may have illustrations of the object they are supposed to represent pinned to their chests.
Props: Desk, books, notepad, Bible, chairs, stethoscope.

(enter receptionist)
Receptionist: Good morning, Dr Fixit. Are you ready for your first appointment?

Dr Fixit: Yes indeed. ***(consults notes)*** It's Penny the Piggybank, isn't it? Show her in. ***(exit receptionist, enter Penny)***

Dr Fixit: Good morning, Penny. Take a seat.

Penny: Good morning, Doctor.

Dr Fixit: Now, tell me, what can I do for you?

Penny: Oh Doctor, you're my last hope. If you can't help me I'll have to give up work. My job is saving money but the trouble is I'm always empty. I never fill up no matter how many coins my owner puts in through my slot.

Dr Fixit: ***(holds stethoscope to Penny's chest)*** Right. Breathe deeply and give yourself a shake. ***(Penny shakes herself)*** Hmm, I see what you mean. You *are* empty. I suspect a hole.

Penny: A hole! Oh Doctor, is that serious... I mean, can you fix it?

Dr Fixit: Of course I can, Penny. All it takes is a bit of sticking plaster. ***(writes on notepad, then gives Penny the note)*** Just take this note through to the treatment room and my assistant will patch you up.

Penny: Thank you so much. I feel better already.

Dr Fixit: Not at all. Next patient, please. ***(enter receptionist and Sam)***

Receptionist: This is Sam the smoke alarm.

Dr Fixit: Good morning, Sam. Take a seat. Now how can I help you?

Sam: ***(hoarsely – pointing at throat)*** It's my voice.

Dr Fixit: Yes, you do sound hoarse.

Sam: I'm supposed to save buildings, Doctor. If a fire breaks out, it's my job to raise the alarm. But how can I do that without a voice?

Dr Fixit: Just stand up for a moment, Sam. I want to run a quick test.

Sam: Will it hurt?

Dr Fixit: No, no… I'm just going to press your red button. All you'll feel is a little push.

(pushes button) There. That didn't hurt, did it?

Sam: ***(rubbing button)*** Not really… so what do you think?

Dr Fixit: I think… no, I'm certain… it's a battery problem. ***(writes on notepad, then gives Sam the note)*** You've lost your voice because your battery's flat. Take this note into the treatment room and my assistant will fix you up with a new one.

Sam: Oh thank you, Doctor. I feel better already.

Dr Fixit: Glad to hear it. ***(exit Sam)*** Next patient, please. ***(enter receptionist and Miles)***

Receptionist: This is Miles the Motorbike.

Dr Fixit: Good morning, Miles. Park yourself over there. Now, how can I help you?

Miles: ***(wearily)*** I've no energy, Doctor. I'm supposed to save time by zooming my owner to work in the morning. But these days I can't zoom anywhere. I haven't the strength to move.

Dr Fixit: Talk to me about your diet.

Miles: What do you want to know?

Dr Fixit: When did you last refuel?

Miles: A couple of weeks ago, maybe. I'm not sure. Is it important?

Dr Fixit: Very. An active motorbike like you needs a high-octane diet. Let me check your tank. Yes… it's no wonder you've got problems. You're running on empty…

Miles: You mean I need a tonic.

Dr Fixit: ***(writing on notepad)*** I mean you need a fuel injection, followed by regular top-ups. ***(gives note to Miles)*** Take this to the treatment room and my assistant will sort you out.

Miles: Vroom… vroom… Thank you, Doctor. I feel better already. Vroom… vroom… vroom… ***(exit Miles)***

Dr Fixit: ***(stands up)*** Well, that was a busy morning. ***(enter receptionist and All Saints Church)***

Receptionist: I'm sorry Doctor Fixit. Another patient has just arrived.

Church: I need to see Dr Fixit. I really need help.

Receptionist: This is All Saints Church… you know, that building from across the road.

Dr Fixit: Goodness! I've never treated a church before. Let me guess… you've a hearing problem. You're suffering from ringing in the steeple.

Church: No, no, it's something much more serious.

Dr Fixit: Take a seat. Tell me your symptoms.

Church: It's my members, Doctor. They're weak. They fall out with each other. They're supposed to save the world and they just can't do it.

Dr Fixit: Save the world, you say. It strikes me that saving money or saving buildings or saving time is a whole lot easier. Saving the world is a HUGE challenge.

Church: ***(sighing)*** Tell me about it...

Dr Fixit: And I don't think there's any point sending you to the treatment room. Sticking plaster wouldn't help. Neither would a new battery or a healthier diet. But wait a minute... ***(stands up and picks up Bible)*** I read of a case like yours in this book. ***(flicks through Bible)*** Yes here we are. A couple of thousand years ago there was a group of Christians with exactly the same complaints as you describe. They were weak... they were fearful... they were supposed to save the world and they hadn't a clue how to go about it.

Church: So what happened?

Dr Fixit: They prayed and waited for God to act, and suddenly the Holy Spirit showered down on them and they were filled with spiritual power.

Church: ***(eagerly)*** Yes, that's it! That's *exactly* what my members need.

Dr Fixit: Well then ***(writing on notepad)***, I advise your members to follow the example of the early church. They should pray and ask God to fill them with power.

Church: But who's going to tell them? I'm a building. People don't listen to buildings. I need a human being to pass the message on... someone like you Doctor. You belong to All Saints.

Dr Fixit: Now hold on a minute... I'm not sure I...

Church: ...please, Doctor, we're talking about saving the world here.

Dr Fixit: Well, I suppose I could come to the next Bible Study. But, you know, just talking about the Holy Spirit won't change things.

Church: I know... I know... but it's a start. Even thinking about God's power makes me excited. You come to the Bible Study, Doctor, and tell the other members what you've just told me. We'll trust the Holy Spirit to do the rest.

APPLICATION

Theme: The power of the Spirit

Explore: The Holy Spirit

The Holy Spirit is God's gift to the Church. In Old Testament times the Holy Spirit was given to a few special people – prophets and kings – to help them to do important jobs. Jesus promised this gift to his disciples (John 14:16-17) and told them to wait for it (Acts 1:4-5). He called the Holy Spirit 'the Counsellor' (John 14:15) meaning that the Holy Spirit would comfort and guide the disciples when Jesus went back to heaven.

The Day of Pentecost

The name Pentecost comes from the Greek word for 'fifty'. It was one of the most important Jewish festivals, held fifty days after the Passover. Today Christians celebrate Pentecost as the day when the first disciples received the gift of the Holy Spirit (Acts 2:1–41). This happened ten days after Jesus went back to heaven (the Ascension). (A retelling of this story is found in *50 Five Minute Stories*, published by Children's Ministry.)

Chat

Chat about imaginary superheroes, e.g. Batman or Superman. What sort of special powers have they? How did they get them? Then talk about the special power God wants us to have. Aim to bring out the fact that the Holy Spirit is God living inside us.

Think

Jesus said, 'Would any of you who are fathers give your son a snake when he asks for fish? Or would you give him a scorpion when he asks for an egg? How much more then will the Father in heaven give the Holy Spirit to those who ask him?' (Luke 11:11–13) Ask the children to think about these words. Have they asked God to fill their lives with his power?

DRAMA 41

THE THREE PILLARS

AGE 10+

SUBJECT: Peter and John heal a lame beggar

BIBLE READING: Acts 3:1–12; 4:1–4

DRAMA NOTES: Suitable for group reading or performance.

Cast: Pillar 1, Pillar 2, Pillar 3.
Staging: The scene is Solomon's Colonnade in Herod's Temple in Jerusalem. The three pillars stand side by side with sleeping Pillar 2 in the centre.

Pillar 2: ***(snoring loudly)*** zzzzzz…zzzzzzz…zzzzzzz…

Pillar 1: ***(to pillar 3)*** I suppose we should wake him?

Pillar 3: Must we? He's a real pain in the arch, the way he goes on. You'd think he was the only pillar in this Temple.

Pillar 1: And that his bit of roof was ten times heavier than ours.

Pillar 2: zzzzz…zzzzzz…zzzzzzz…

Pillar 1: Mind you the longer he sleeps, the harder it's going to be to explain things. I mean, he's missed out on all the excitement.

Pillar 3: Probably just as well. He *hates* excitement.

Pillar 1: And noise.

Pillar 3: And change.

Pillar 1: Still, with all the extra people we've had on our steps, he really ought to check himself for cracks.

Pillar 3: Oh, all right then. Let's wake him. After three… one, two, three…

Pillars 1 & 3: Wakey, wakey, Brother Pillar!

Pillar 2: ***(waking up)*** What was that?… What did you say?

Pillar 1: We were just saying, you've missed out on the excitement.

Pillar 2: Excitement! What excitement? This is the Temple. There shouldn't be any excitement.

Pillar 1: But people can't help getting excited about miracles, Brother.

Pillar 3: And while you were asleep, a miracle happened right under our roof – just over there beside the Beautiful Gate.

Pillar 1: You remember that lame beggar who always sat there with his begging bowl. Well, a couple of days ago, just before the three o'clock prayers, two followers of Jesus healed him.

Pillar 3: One of them looked him straight in the eyes and said, 'In the name of Jesus Christ, walk.' Then they pulled him to his feet…

Pillar 1: ...and he walked. In fact, he didn't just walk, he *jumped!*

Pillar 3: He came racing up our steps, praising God at the top of his voice.

Pillar 2: Disgraceful! Running and jumping and shouting in the Temple. He ought to have sat down quietly and got on with his begging.

Pillar 1: I don't think you understand, Brother. He didn't need to beg any more. He'd been…

Pillar 2: ***(interrupts)*** …I understand a threat to our traditions when I hear one. Those followers of Jesus are always stirring people up.

Pillar 1: You're right there. After the healing, a *huge* crowd gathered on our steps.

Pillar 3: And Peter – the one who healed the beggar – he preached and told them all they needed to put their faith in Jesus.

Pillar 2: Put their faith in… I don't *believe* it… Why didn't the Temple Guards stop him?

Pillar 1: Well, there was such a crowd they didn't want to interfere.

Pillar 2: Oh, wonderful! Here we are with followers of Jesus preaching a new religion and our Temple Guard just stand around turning a blind eye. Mark my words… they'll live to regret this…

Pillar 1: ...calm down, Brother. The Temple Guard did their duty. As soon as the religious leaders gave the word, they put Peter and John under arrest.

Pillar 2: Oh... right... I see... The followers of Jesus were arrested, were they? ***(yawns)*** Oh well, I suppose that does put a different slant on things. Jail's the place for them. And if the Temple Guard have any sense, they'll send that beggar back to his begging. Break his legs. Yes. That's the way to get everything back to normal. ***(yawns again)*** Nice, dull normal. Nobody getting healed. Nobody getting saved. Nothing changing. Ever... ***(falls asleep)*** zzzzz...zzzz...zzz...

Pillar 3: He's gone back to sleep.

Pillar 1: And he still doesn't know that Peter and John walked free...

Pillar 3: ...or that they've refused to stop preaching...

Pillar 1: ...or that after the healing, over 5000 people became followers of Jesus.

Pillar 3: So are we going to wake him up and tell him?

Pillar 1: What do you think? ***(they both look at Pillar 2)***

Pillar 2: zzzz...zzzzz...zzzzzz...

Pillar 3: ***(smiles)*** I just remembered something. The other day a sparrow asked me whether I woke up grumpy in the morning.

Pillar 2: zzzzzz...zzzzzz...zzzzz...

Pillar 1: And you said...

Pillar 3: ...'Yes, of course – now and again. But mostly we just let him sleep on!'

APPLICATION

Theme: Expecting God to act

Explore: The Book of Acts

The book of Acts tells the story of what happened after Jesus' resurrection. It was written by Luke, a Greek doctor, who also wrote the Gospel of Luke. Luke travelled with the apostles for at least thirty years and was able to write a first-hand account of the growth of the early church. In this action-packed account, the 'acts' of the title can be seen as the actions of the apostles and of the Holy Spirit who gave them power.

Peter

Simon Peter was a born leader. Jesus told him that he would play a major role in founding the church (Matthew 16:18). Before this happened, Peter had a lot to learn. During Jesus' trial he denied that he knew Jesus three times to avoid being arrested (Matthew 26:69–75). But after Pentecost he preached fearlessly and won thousands of people to Christ. Two books in the New Testament (1 and 2 Peter) were written by him.

Chat

Remind the group what the grumpy pillar said about getting the Temple back to normal – 'Nice dull normal. Nobody getting healed. Nobody getting saved. Nothing changing. Ever.' Chat about how the story of Peter and John healing the lame beggar shows what was 'normal' for the first Christians. What is spiritually normal for us?

Think

Discuss the question, 'Do we come to worship expecting God to act?'

DRAMA 42

AGE 8+

SUBJECT: **Peter preaches to the Gentiles**

BIBLE READING: **Acts 10:34-35, 44-47**

DRAMA NOTES: This is a parable story where the focus is on the actors' clenched fists.

Cast: Two narrators, four actors (Chief Fist, 2 Farmer Fists and Friend Fist) to mime the story.
Staging: Narrators together stage right. There is a cardboard box (stage right) with a notice on the side away from the audience saying, 'If the treasure you would own, you must throw away your stone.' There is a small table and chair for the Chief Fist to sit on stage left. Fists all have their hands clenched round stones (made of playdough!)
Costumes: Actors wear gloves – white gloves for Chief Fist, rubber gloves for Farmer Fists, coloured gloves for Friend Fist. Otherwise they are dressed in black.
Props: Gloves, playdough stones, box to represent treasure chest, chair, CD player and instrumental CD.

Narrator 1: There was once a tribe of warriors known as the Fists. ***(enter Chief Fist and Farmer Fists who raise clenched fists as if about to fight)***

Narrator 2: The Fists all marched around holding stones… ***(Fists open and shut hands to reveal stones)*** to make themselves hard. ***(Fists punch air)***

Narrator 1: And they believed they'd been promised a treasure that would fill them with power. ***(Fists flex muscles – Chief Fist sits on throne)***

Narrator 2: Then, one day, two Farmer Fists found a treasure chest on their land. ***(Farmer Fists move stage right and discover box)***

Narrator 1: On its side was a sign, which read *'If this Treasure you would own, you must throw away your stone.'* ***(Farmer Fist 2 turns box round without unclenching fists)***

Narrator 2: When the farmers saw the chest, they got *really* excited. ***(Farmer Fists pump fists in the air)***

Narrator 1: They were sure they'd found the treasure promised to their ancestors.

Narrator 2: So they took the chest to the Chief Fist. ***(Farmer Fists push chest towards Chief on throne)***

Narrator 1: But when the Chief Fist read the chest's message, he was furious. ***(Chief Fist thumps table)***

Narrator 2: 'The treasure promised to our ancestors was meant to make us strong. Throwing away our stones will make us weak,' he cried. 'This chest has been sent to deceive us.' ***(Chief Fist thumps table again – Farmer Fists move quickly back across stage)***

Narrator 1: The Chief Fist decided that the chest must be destroyed.

Narrator 2: So he smashed it…***(Chief Fist batters the chest)***

Narrator 1: …and dumped it in a quarry. ***(Chief Fist knocks box off stage)***

Narrator 2: Then he gave orders that on no account were any Fists to throw away their stones. ***(Chief Fist points and shakes index fingers at Farmer Fists in a commanding gesture)***

Narrator 1: Still, the Farmer Fists couldn't forget the chest's message. ***(Farmer Fists clasp heads in fists)***

Narrator 2: The more they thought of it, the more they wanted to do what it said.

Narrator 1: Until finally they could hold back no longer.

Narrator 2: They unclenched their fingers and let their stones go. ***(Farmer Fists open their hands and drop stone)***

Narrator 1: And an amazing thing happened. ***(music plays)***

Narrator 2: For the first time ever, the Fists felt free. ***(Farmer Fists flex hands and wiggle fingers)***

Narrator 1: They were able to do things they could never have done before. ***(Farmer Fists move to the centre of the stage and play clapping game)***

Narrator 2: Of course, it wasn't long before the Chief Fist found out what had happened. ***(Chief Fist gets up and moves towards Farmer Fists in a threatening manner)*** Immediately, he placed the Farmer Fists under arrest. ***(Chief Fist marches round farmers, shaking index finger at them)*** 'I will destroy you, just as I destroyed the chest,' he raged. And he marched them to the quarry. ***(Chief Fist uses finger and arm like a sword to prod Farmer Fists to the side of the stage)***

Narrator 1: But when they got there, they found that the quarry had been filled in! ***(Chief Fist leaps back in shock – Farmer Fists gesture excitedly)***

Narrator 2: In place of the ugly crater, there was a beautiful rose garden. ***(Farmer Fists sniff the air)***

Narrator 1: The Chief Fist was so shocked, he went straight back to his palace and spent the rest of his days trying to work out what had happened. ***(Chief Fist flops into seat, holding head between fists)***

Narrator 2: The Farmer Fists, meanwhile, were keener than ever to share the good news. ***(enter Friend Fist stage left. Farmer Fists run to meet him/her)***

Narrator 1: 'We've received the treasure promised to our ancestors and you can receive it too,' they cried. ***(Farmer Fists gesture and wave)***

Narrator 2: The next thing, lots of Fists were throwing away their stones. ***(Friend Fist drops stones – plays clapping game with Farmer Fists)***

Narrator 1: Soon there were so many happy, stone-free Fists in the land that they became known by a new name.

Narrator 2: Hands. ***(Farmer Fists and Friend Fist place hands together as if praying)***

Narrator 1: And that isn't the end of the story…

Narrator 2: …for the Hands made another discovery. ***(Fists wave excitedly)***

Narrator 1: They discovered that the power they'd received wasn't just for members of their own tribe. It was for members of other tribes too.

Narrator 2: They became Treasure-sharers, leaving their land to bring their message to Feet and Eyes and Ears all over the world. ***(Fists point to different body parts)***

Narrator 1: And before long they were part of a worldwide body. ***(Fists join hands, hold them up in the air and bow)***

APPLICATION

Theme: Discovery

Explore: The Gentiles

The word Gentiles means 'nations'. For the descendants of Abraham and Jacob it meant people who came from any nation other than Israel i.e. non-Jews. Jews set themselves apart from Gentiles by not marrying them, by keeping to certain rules about food and diet and by their menfolk being circumcised. The prophets promised that the Messiah would be a light to the Gentiles (Isaiah 42:6, Luke 2:32) but, to begin with, the first Jewish Christians only shared their faith with their fellow Jews. Soon God showed that this new faith was for everyone. Gentiles as well as Jews received the Holy Spirit and were baptised.

Chat

Watch a discovery scene from a video (e.g. the scene in *Finding Nemo* when the Turtles discover that Marlin has swum all the way from the Barrier Reef in search of his son). Chat about a time when you have discovered something that changed the way you thought. Then chat about how Peter's discovery changed the way he thought about Gentiles.

Think

Ask the children to think about discoveries they have made as Christians – discoveries about God's love, about forgiveness, about the power of the Holy Spirit. Picture these discoveries as spiritual treasure. Are they sharing their treasure with others?

DRAMA 43

A MAN CALLED ANN

AGE 9+

SUBJECT: Saul and Ananias

BIBLE READING: Acts 9:10-18

DRAMA NOTES: Suitable for performance by adults for children, by confident children, or using puppets.

Cast: Max, Mum.
Props: Schoolbag.

(Max walks in, carrying schoolbag)
Mum: How was your day?

Max: Rotten.

Mum: Why? What happened?

Max: I wrote a poem about this guy we've been doing in RE… the one who healed Saul's eyes after Jesus spoke to him on the road to Damascus.

Mum: Ananias.

Max: Yeah. Him.

Mum: So what's so rotten about that?

Max: Miss Knight wants me to read the poem out in assembly… and I don't want to. Not in front of … you know… *everyone.* I need you to write a note, Mum. Tell her I've lost my voice or something.

Mum: Let's hear the poem first.

Max: Aw, *Mum!* ***(takes paper from pocket)***

Mum: Please…

Max: Oh, all right. ***(unfolds paper)*** Here goes:
Ann, he was a Christian.
Damascus was his home.
His real name, Ananias
is too long for this poem.

Mum: Good start. Carry on…

Max:
One day God gave a job to Ann
which came as a surprise.
God said, 'Saul's round at Judas' house.
Go there and heal his eyes.'

Mum: Excellent!

Max: Oh help! Oh dear! Oh pants!' cried Ann.
This job filled him with woe.
He knew Saul hated Christians.
He didn't want to go.

Mum: Hmmm...

Max: Well, I'm sure he *didn't.* I mean the job stank. Saul was a Pharisee and he'd been coming to Damascus to arrest Christians. For all Ann knew, the minute he got his sight back he might have turned round and arrested *him.*

Mum: Yes. All right. Let's move on to the next verse.

Max: Then God told Ann that Saul had changed
and would win loads of races...

Mum: Races! No – you've definitely got the wrong idea there. The Bible tells us Saul made long missionary journeys, but he never ran races.

Max: I'm not talking about athletic type races, I'm talking about races of people:

Then God told Ann that Saul had changed
And would win loads of races
of people who would follow Christ
in lots of different places.

OK? Get it?

Mum: ***(nodding)*** I get it.

Max: So Ann, he did as he was told.
He laid hands on Saul that day;
and Saul, he got his eyesight back
and was baptised straight away.

Mum: ***(encouragingly)*** That's good.

Max: Punching the air, Ann whooped and cried,
'God has changed Saul's heart.'
Then, as he'd starved for three whole days,
Saul ate some rhubarb tart.

(Mum shakes head)
Max: No?

Mum: No.

Max: What's wrong with it?

Mum: The tart. The Bible doesn't say anything about rhubarb tart. It hadn't been invented.

Max: All right… all right… I'll drop the tart. Just give me a word to rhyme with food.

Mum: Rude… mood…

Max: That's it!
Then, as he'd starved for three whole days,
Saul went and ate some food.
He needed strength to build the church
now God had changed his mood. OK?

Mum: Well, God did change a bit more than Saul's mood… but we'll call it poetic license.

Max: Last verse, then.
This story's in the Book of Acts
and I learnt something through it.
If God gives me a risky job,
then I should go and do it.

Mum: You don't mean that.

Max: Yes I do.

Mum: Seriously.

Max: Yes.

Mum: So why won't you read your poem out in assembly?

Max: Because... well... because... the other guys might... oh, I see... all right! I'll do it.

APPLICATION

Theme: Links in a chain

Explore: Saul

Saul (who later became known by his Greek name, Paul) was a Greek-speaking Jew. He became a Pharisee and prided himself on keeping the Law in every detail. To begin with, his beliefs made him persecute Christians. Acts 6:58 tells us that he was present, supporting the Jews, when they killed Stephen, the first Christian martyr. Then on his way to persecute Christians in Damascus, Saul met Jesus and his whole life changed (Acts 9:1-8). He went on to become one of the most important leaders in the early church.

Chat

Give out strips of paper and glue. Working individually or in pairs challenge the children to see who can produce the longest paper chain in two minutes. Then ask if anyone can see a connection between a chain and the Bible story. Talk about how Ananias was a link in the chain, linking Saul to Jesus. Saul went on to link many more people to Christ. Point out how sometimes it can feel risky to be a link... a bit like leaning down over the edge of a cliff to pull someone else to safety. But if we know that Jesus is on the other side, holding firmly onto us, then we can reach out safely.

Think

Think about people who link us to Jesus. Thank God for them. Ask him to help us be that link for others.

DRAMA 44

PRAISE POWER

AGE 6+

SUBJECT: **Paul and Silas in prison**

BIBLE READING: **Acts 16:22-34**

DRAMA NOTES: A simple drama for performance by young children using percussion instruments.

Cast: Narrator.

Thwack! Thwack! Thwack! Thwack! ***(castanets)***
The whip comes down on the prisoner's back.
Paul gets beaten, Silas too.
The whipping leaves them black and blue.
Thwack! Thwack! Thwack! ***(castanets)***

Sing! Sing! Sing! Sing! ***(triangle or glockenspiel)***
Two prisoners do the strangest thing.
Paul and Silas do not cry.
Instead they pray to God on high.
Sing! Sing! Sing! ***(triangle or glockenspiel)***

Rumble…rumble…rumble…rumble… ***(drum)***
The earthquake makes the prison crumble.
It's acting like a master key
setting Paul and Silas free.
Rumble…rumble…rumble… ***(drum)***

Hush! Hush! Hush! Hush!
Paul and Silas do not rush.
They wait and save the jailor's life.
He trusts in God. So does his wife.
Hush! Hush! Hush!

Hooray! Hooray! Hooray! Hooray! ***(castanets, triangle, drum and cymbals)***
God has answered prayer today.
A miracle has happened here.
Paul and Silas clap and cheer.
Hooray! Hooray! Hooray! ***(castanets, triangle, drum and cymbals)***

APPLICATION

Theme: Being thankful

Explore: Philippi

Paul made three missionary journeys, teaching and preaching about Jesus. The story retold here happened on his second missionary journey, when he visited the city of Philippi. Paul started a church there - the jailer and his family must have been among the first members. Later, when Paul was in prison in Rome, he wrote a letter to his friends in that church (Philippians 1:1).

Chat

Chat about what happened to Paul and Silas in Philippi. Ask what was surprising about the way Paul and Silas acted. Draw a picture of a smiley face and write the words underneath, 'Always be thankful to God.' Say that this was something Paul wrote in a letter to some of his Christian friends (1 Thessalonians 5:18) and he wrote it because he knew that no matter what happened God was in control.

Think

Talk about things to thank God for. Construct a short prayer including everyone's ideas.

DRAMA 45

THE LIGHT KEEPERS

AGE 11+

SUBJECT: **Paul teaches about life in the Spirit**

BIBLE READING: **Romans 13:11-14**

DRAMA NOTES: Suitable for group reading or performance by confident actors.

Cast: Gabriel, Major Drum, Apple Drum, Fido the dog.
Staging: The setting is a lighthouse. Narrator is centre stage in front of table: Fido is in a dog basket stage right. Major Drum, reading a newspaper, and his daughter Apple, reading a magazine, are seated on either side of a table with two CD players between them. On another table is a box with a bright red button labelled, 'Emergency Generator'.
Props: Dog basket, box labelled Emergency Generator, table, chairs, newspaper, magazine, 2 CD players, CD of brass band music, CD of rock music, bag with two MP3 players, triangle (or other means of sounding an alarm).

Gabriel: Ladies and Gentlemen, welcome on board ship for our special End Times cruise. My name is Gabriel. And I'm hosting this evening's onboard entertainment. Now, those of you sitting on my left, please take a look through your portholes. What do you see? That's right. A flashing beacon. That beacon, Ladies and Gentlemen belongs to End Times Lighthouse. And I, for one, am very glad it's there, guiding our ship through the treacherous waters of End Times Strait. Yes, Ladies and Gentlemen, we owe a lot to that lighthouse, and we've a special surprise for you this evening. We're going to visit it, and you won't even have to leave your seats. As we speak, a special cable is linking us to the lighthouse living-room. And look! ***(moves stage left and points)*** There are the Light Keepers – Major Roger Drum and his daughter Apple. Give them a wave. Hi there, Roger. This is Gabe, speaking from on board the Tabernacle. Are you receiving me? ***(Major Roger and Apple keep reading, Fido snores)*** *Are you receiving me*? ***(pauses)*** Oh dear! It looks like I'm not going to get a chance to say 'roger, Roger' after all. We can see the Light Keepers but they can't see us… You might say we've just become flies on the Lighthouse wall. ***(Apple and Major turn over pages of their magazine and newspaper)*** So I suppose this is where I do my fly on the wall impression. ***(flaps around)*** zzzzz… zzzzz… zzzzzzzz. No, seriously folks, this is where we make the most of the chance to watch the Light Keepers' work. ***(pauses)*** Hah! It's a bit like watching paint dry, isn't it. Of course we know Major Roger and Apple may not look that busy, but really they're doing a vital job. They're alert. They're listening out. It's up to them to make sure that the beacon we just saw stays lit and keeps guiding us. So the Major and Apple are always listening out for the sound of an alarm. Yes, folks you could say that listening out is their number one duty. ***(Fido whines)***

Major Drum: Did you hear something?

Apple: It's Fido. He wants to be fed.

Major Drum: So – *feed* him.

Apple: I'm busy.

Major Drum: No, you're not. Feed the *dog*. ***(Fido whines)***

Apple: In a minute. ***(Apple turns on CD player and rock music fills the air. Apple starts jigging in her seat)***

Major Drum: Turn that racket *off.* You know we're meant to be listening.

Apple: ***(turns music down slightly)*** It isn't a racket. It's my favourite band.

Major Drum: Band! You can't call that a band! Any band worth its salt has trumpets and trombones. And as for the drummer... he's all over the place. Here, let's have a *proper* band. ***(turns off rock and roll music. Turns on second CD player and starts band music. Major beats time on table)***

Apple: For goodness' sake, Dad. You're so sad! ***(Apple turns volume of band music right down)***

Major Drum: How dare you! ***(turns band music volume back up)***

Apple: Two can play at that game. ***(turns up rock music and jigs about)***

(Major Drum turns down both CD players)

Major Drum: Sit down, Apple. You're being very silly. You *know* we can't both listen to different music at the same time.

Apple: Yes, we can.

Major Drum: No, we can't.

Apple: Yes we can – if we use these. ***(takes MP3 players out of bag)***

Major Drum: Now Apple, we're Light Keepers, remember. What if the emergency alarm goes off? We're not supposed to do anything that could block out the sound.

Apple: Loosen up, Dad. The emergency alarm hasn't gone off in months.

Major Drum: Oh, all right then. ***(they put on headphones. Major starts marching on spot. Apple starts dancing)***

Gabriel: I'm sorry, Ladies and Gentlemen, I'll try and get their attention. Major Roger... Apple... This is Gabe calling from The Tabernacle. Are you receiving me? ***(alarm sounds)*** Oh no! It's the alarm. Don't panic, Ladies and Gentlemen. Just take a look through the starboard portholes. Can you see the Lighthouse beacon? No? Now keep calm, everyone. We may be sailing through a treacherous stretch of water without a safety beacon, but the Light Keepers will activate the generator. ***(alarm keeps ringing, Major continues marching, Apple continues jigging)*** I repeat, Major Roger... Apple... you must *activate* the *generator*. ***(Fido howls)*** They're useless. They can't hear a thing. Please don't panic, Ladies and Gentleman. Our ship is doomed... but please *keep calm*... ***(Fido races over to the emergency generator and pushes the button. Alarm stops)*** Thank goodness. ***(wipes brow)*** Yes, you're telling me the light's back on. We can all take a deep breath and relax. The emergency is over. But I promise you as soon as the Captain hears about this, that dog will get a medal and those two so-called Light Keepers will get *the sack*.

APPLICATION

Theme: Being spiritually alert

Explore: Paul's letters

As well as travelling around preaching about Jesus, Paul wrote letters to the Christians in the churches he started. His letters make up 13 books of the New Testament. They were often written during or after one of his journeys and were handed into the church by one of his messengers. Paul's letters all give encouragement, warnings and advice about living the Christian life.

Chat

Chat about the Light Keepers' actions in the drama. What was wrong with their behaviour? Bring out the fact that they stopped paying attention and didn't do their job. Then read Romans 13:11-14. What sort of behaviour shows that Christians are alert spiritually? What sort of behaviour shows that they are not?

Think

Suggest that a hidden camera has recorded everything group members have said and done for the last 24 hours. How would they feel about others seeing the recording?

DRAMA 46

EQUIPPED

AGE 11+

SUBJECT: **Paul teaches about spiritual armour**

BIBLE READING: **Ephesians 6:14–17**

DRAMA NOTES: Best performed for an all-age group.

Cast: Two narrators, Christy.
Staging: A box on stage with a Bible behind it or in it.
Props: Box, Bible, rucksack containing safety harness, helmet, sun glasses, boots and gloves.

Narrator 1: Christy was a Christian, keen to live God's way. ***(enter Christy wearing backpack)***
She set off on life's journey, following Jesus every day.
And then – oh dear – things went wrong. What was she to do?
A giant problem blocked her path, with no way round or through. ***(Christy pretends to come up against barrier)***
This mountain of a problem seemed sure to turn her back. ***(Christy turns round)***
But then the Spirit whispered...

Narrator 2: ...'Take a look in your rucksack.' ***(Christy takes off rucksack)***

Narrator 1: Christy opened up the bag and set it on the ground. ***(opens rucksack)***
She started to unpack it. And this is what she found:
First, a safety harness – the sort that climbers wear – ***(puts on harness)***
with straps and belts and rings for ropes, to hold them in the air.

Narrator 2: 'You're safe when harnessed to the truth, '...

Narrator 1: ...the Holy Spirit said.

Narrator 2: 'The truth that Jesus lived and died and rose up from the dead.'

Narrator 1: Next Christy found a pair of boots – soft, yet tough and strong. ***(puts on boots)***
The Spirit spoke again, as she bent down to put them on.

Narrator 2: 'Those who share God's love wear boots which carry them along.'

Narrator 1: Then came gloves. The moment Christy pulled these on her hands ***(puts on gloves)*** they filled her heart with courage to tackle big demands.

Narrator 2: 'Keep serving God,'...

Narrator 1: ...the Spirit breathed...

Narrator 2: ...'Always do what's right.
Honesty's the secret of inner strength and might.'

Narrator 1: Next came a helmet for her head. With it, she felt secure. ***(puts on helmet)*** She knew, whatever happened, God's love for her was sure.
And then she found some glasses – well, this was a surprise. ***(picks up sunglasses)*** they acted like a shield and filtered out the devil's lies. ***(puts on sunglasses)***
She put them on and saw the path ahead through different eyes.
Amazingly she now could see a choice of climbing routes.
Now she had her harness, glasses, helmet, gloves and boots. ***(points to different pieces of equipment)***

Narrator 2 'Don't go yet,'...

Narrator 1: ...the Spirit breathed...

Narrator 2: ...'Don't hurry. Take your time.
Look closely at that mountain before you start to climb.'

Narrator 1: Christy looked. ***(peers upwards)*** Hey, what was that! ***(waves excitedly)***
The sight filled her with hope.
A figure on the summit was letting down a rope. ***(Christy moves forward and takes Bible from hiding place)***
The Spirit said...

Narrator 2: ...'That rope's God's word. His power will pull you through.
As you climb, hold onto it and he'll hold onto you.' ***(Christy holds up Bible)***

APPLICATION

Theme: Beating problems

Explore: Spiritual battles

Paul warned Christians to expect problems. He himself had to cope with difficult people (2 Timothy 4:14) and lots of difficult circumstances (2 Corinthians 11:23–29). Paul taught that Satan opposed God's work and was out to create problems for Christians (Ephesians 6:10–12). He also taught Christians how they could win through (Ephesians 6:14–17, 2 Thessalonians 3:1–3).

Chat

Talk with the group about their ideas of who Satan is and the sort of problems he creates. Suggest that there are two traps Satan wants us to fall in to. Trap one is to believe he doesn't exist, so we don't guard against him. Trap two is to believe he is more powerful than he really is, so we start seeing him everywhere. Then look at the equipment God gives us for defeating Satan – knowledge of Christian truth, being sure of our salvation, the desire to spread the Good News, right living, faith that God's in control and experience of the power of his word.

Think

Copy out the words of 1 Corinthians 15:57. 'But thanks be to God. He gives us the victory through our Lord Jesus Christ.' Praise God for the victory that is ours in Christ.

DRAMA 47

THE FAIREST OF ALL

AGE 8+

SUBJECT: **Paul teaches about fairness**

BIBLE READING: **Colossians 4:1**

DRAMA NOTES: Suitable for group reading or performance.

Cast: Two narrators, Queen, Flo White, dwarf.
Staging: Narrators side by side stage left. There should be a plastic bin, a table and a couple of stools set at an angle centre stage.
Props: Table, two chairs, plastic bin, crown, apple, banana, bottle marked poison, small mirror, hat, two mugs, tray, fair trade coffee, envelope.

Narrator 1: Once upon a time there was a wicked queen who was as vain as she was beautiful. ***(Queen puts on crown, and tries it at several different angles)*** Every day she would gaze into her magic mirror and say: ***(Queen holds up pocket mirror)***

Narrator 2: Mirror, mirror off the wall,
who's the fairest of them all?

Narrator 1: And the mirror would reply:

Narrator 2: Thou, O Queen, art the fairest of all. ***(Queen sets down mirror and smiles)***

Narrator 1: But one day when the queen asked her question: ***(Queen picks up mirror)***

Narrator 2: Mirror, mirror off the wall,
Who's the fairest of them all?

Narrator 1: The mirror replied:

Narrator 2: Thou, O Queen, art lovely to see,
but Flo White the grocer is fairer than thee. ***(Queen stamps in anger)***

Narrator 1: Unable to stand the thought of anyone being more beautiful than she was, the wicked queen decided to get rid of her rival. ***(Queen rubs chin)***

Narrator 2: So she came up with a cunning plan. ***(Queen signals a bright idea)*** She ran out into her orchard... ***(exit Queen)***

Narrator 1: ...picked a rosy red apple from an apple tree... ***(Queen comes back in with an apple)***

Narrator 2: ...injected the apple with poison... ***(Queen tampers with apple)***

Narrator 1: ...disguised herself as an apple grower... ***(Queen puts on hat over crown)***

Narrator 2: ...and set off to poison Flo White. ***(Queen walks round stage)***

Narrator 1: When she reached the grocer's shop... ***(enter dwarf stage left who stands behind table)*** she found a dwarf behind the counter busily serving customers.

Narrator 1: The wicked queen set her apple on the counter and said...

Narrator 2: ...'I am an apple-grower. I've brought one of my apples for your mistress.'

Narrator 1: The dwarf turned round and called...

Narrator 2: ...'Miss White, there's an apple-grower here to see you.'

Narrator 1: A moment later, in came a plain, wrinkled, old lady... ***(enter Flo White)***

Narrator 2: ...who picked up the apple and said... ***(Flo picks up apple)***

Narrator 1: ...'Hello. I'm Flo White. How can I help you?'

Narrator 2: The wicked Queen was so shocked by Miss White's age and lack of beauty...

Narrator 1: ...that her poisoning plan went right out of her head and she muttered...

Narrator 2: ...'I want to buy a banana.'

Narrator 1: Smilingly, Flo handed her one. ***(Flo hands Queen banana)*** And that was when the wicked queen noticed the Fairtrade sticker on its skin.

Narrator 2: 'Fairtrade!'...

Narrator 1: ...she cried.

Narrator 2: 'What does that mean?'

Narrator 1: 'Fairtrade is a charity set up to make sure that growers in poorer countries are paid fairly for their crops,'...

Narrator 2: ...Flo White explained.

Narrator 1: 'This shop is a Fairtrade shop which means the worker who grew that banana has been paid a fair price for his fruit.'

Narrator 2: Suddenly, the wicked queen understood the magic mirror's words.

Narrator 1: Flo White wasn't fair to look at. She was someone who treated people fairly.

Narrator 2: Immediately the queen tried to snatch the poisoned apple out of her hand. ***(Queen lunges towards Flo)*** But it was too late.

Narrator 1: Flo bit into the poisoned apple, clasped her throat and started to choke. ***(exit Flo, staggering and clutching her throat – stage left. Dwarf runs after her. Queen holds hands to head and knocks hat and crown off)***

Narrator 2: 'Alas! What have I done?'...

Narrator 1: ...the wicked queen shrieked.

Narrator 2: And she fled from the scene of the crime. ***(Queen runs off stage right – dwarf runs on, picks up hat and crown and runs off again)***

Narrator 1: Back in the palace, the wicked queen told her magic mirror exactly what she thought of it. ***(enter Queen with mirror)***

Narrator 2: 'You misled me,'...

Narrator 1: ...she cried.

Narrator 2: 'And now I've gone and poisoned the fairest grocer in the land.'

Narrator 1: To show how sorry she was, the wicked queen threw the mirror away... ***(Queen puts mirror into bin)***

Narrator 2: …and laced her banana with poison. ***(Queen takes out poison)***

Narrator 1: She was about to eat it when she heard a knock at the door. ***(knocking sound)***

Narrator 2: 'Who's there?'…

Narrator 1: …cried the Queen.

Narrator 2: Surprise! Surprise! It was Flo White and her dwarf. ***(enter Flo White and dwarf)***

Narrator 1: They had come to return the wicked Queen's crown. ***(dwarf hands over crown)***

Narrator 2: And to invite her to a wedding. ***(Flo gives Queen envelope)***

Narrator 1: 'I'm marrying the handsome doctor who saved my life when I choked on that apple of yours,'…

Narrator 2: …said Flo White.

Narrator 1: ***(Flo clasps hands)*** 'We fell in love the moment I got my breath back. And it's all thanks to you.'

Narrator 2: At this, the wicked queen decided not to poison herself after all. ***(Queen tosses banana in bin)***

Narrator 1: She hugged Flo White. ***(Queen hugs Flo)*** And vowed to stop being wicked and to rule her country well.

Narrator 2: 'I shall make this land a Fairtrade land'…

Narrator 1: …she declared.

Narrator 1: Then she and Flo sat down to discuss their future plans… ***(Flo and Queen sit down at table – exit dwarf)*** while the dwarf made them a nice hot drink.

Narrator 2: Of Fairtrade coffee, of course. ***(Enter dwarf with mugs on tray)***

APPLICATION

Theme: Faith in action

Explore: Service

The Bible teaches that real faith is seen in action – in the way God's people treat others, especially those who are poor. The Old Testament prophets said this (Isaiah 58:3,6–7; Jeremiah 7:5–7). So did John the Baptist (Luke 3:11–14) and Jesus (Luke 11:46). Paul also taught that loving Jesus should make people want to treat others fairly.

Chat

Bring in some Fairtrade products (bananas, chocolate, coffee, tea) and let the children sample them. Show them the Fairtrade logo and explain a bit more about what the organisation does (see www.fairtrade.org.uk for information). Chat about where these products can be bought locally. Make posters encouraging people to use them.

Think

About those who live in poverty. Pray that God inspires more and more people to take the sort of action that will help them.

DRAMA 48

JACK AND THE NEW-MAKER

AGE 8+

SUBJECT: **Paul teaches about being made new**

BIBLE READING: **2 Corinthians 4:16-18**

DRAMA NOTES: Suitable for group reading or performance. To add an interactive element to the performance, ask the audience to moo every time they hear the word 'cow'.

Cast: Narrator (adult), Jack, grandmother, tramp, Daisy the Cow – optional.
Staging: The narrator sits stage right reading from a book of fairy stories (script may be hidden inside). There is a small table and stool stage left.
Props: Table, stool, sign with the words 'smelly cheese for sale' on one side and 'closed' on the other, baggy jacket for tramp, shoe-box, two wrapped cheese slices, sock with coins inside, bucket.

Narrator: Jack and his granny and Daisy lived together in the country. ***(enter grandmother on stick, Jack with bucket and Daisy)*** Jack was young and active. Granny was old and lame. And Daisy was a *cow*. ***(audience moo)*** Every day Daisy the *cow...* ***(audience moo)*** gave lots of milk... ***(Jack hands bucket to granny)*** which Jack's granny made into her own brand of extra smelly cheese and sold from a little stall in their front garden. ***(grandmother props up notice 'Smelly Cheese for Sale' and sits down at table)***

Then out of the blue, Daisy the *cow...* ***(audience moo)*** disappeared. Jack looked everywhere... ***(Jack mimes searching)*** but he couldn't find her. With no milk to make into cheese... ***(Jack holds bucket upside down)*** Granny had to shut up shop. ***(grandmother turns round notice to show 'Closed' sign and Jack puts bucket under table)*** By the end of the week, they were down to their last cheese slice. ***(grandmother holds up cheese slice, Jack rubs tummy)*** Granny said, 'We'll have to get a new *cow*,' ***(audience moo)*** and she gave Jack all their savings... ***(grandmother gives Jack coins in a sock)*** and sent him to the market to buy one.

Jack set out, nibbling the last cheese slice as he went. ***(exit grandmother. Jack walks around stage, eating cheese)*** He hadn't walked very far when he met a tramp. ***(enter tramp)***

'Hello, Jack. Where are you off to?' asked the tramp. ***(tramp addresses Jack)*** 'I'm off to market to buy a new *cow,'* ***(audience moo)*** Jack replied. ***(Jack holds up sock)***

'In that case, it's your lucky day. I'm selling something very special and you've got the money to buy it.' From inside his jacket, the tramp produced a box.

'What's so special about that?' asked Jack. ***(Jack puts sock away)***

'You won't find another box like this anywhere in the world,' replied the tramp.

'It's a hundred times more useful than a *cow*. ***(audience moo)*** You could say that *cows...* ***(audience moo)*** are moo-makers but this box is a new-maker.'

'A new-maker?' Jack scratched his head. ***(Jack scratches head)*** 'What's that?'

'It's an incredible machine that makes half-eaten things whole and worn-out things new,' said the tramp. 'Here give me your cheese.' The tramp put the cheese into the new-maker… ***(tramp pretends to put wrapper into box but actually hides it in his pocket)*** counted to ten… ***(tramp counts on fingers)*** then opened the box and came out with… ***(tramp puts hand into box and produces new cheese slice)*** a brand new cheese slice.

'Wow!' cried Jack. 'That's amazing!' ***(Jack holds up hands in surprise. Tramp hands him cheese)***

'I'll show you something even more amazing,' said the tramp. ***(Jack pockets cheese slice and takes out sock of money)*** 'The new-maker works on people as well as things.'

'How do you mean?' cried Jack.

'Watch me!' ***(tramp sets down box and takes off jacket)*** The tramp took off his jacket and did five press-ups and a backward roll. ***(tramp does press-ups and backward roll)***

'Last week, I could hardly move I was so lame,' he said. ***(tramp puts jacket on again)*** 'Then I stood with the new-maker on my head for ten minutes and now I'm good as new.'

'Wow!' cried Jack. 'My granny could do with a new-maker.'

'It's yours for a sock full of silver,' said the tramp.

'Done,' said Jack. ***(Jack gives sock to tramp)***

'Quite so,' said the tramp, and off he went. ***(exit tramp)***
Excitedly Jack raced home with his prize. 'Granny...' he yelled. 'Granny! Granny! Wait till you see what I've bought...' ***(enter grandmother. Jack holds out box)***

Oh dear! When Granny saw the new-maker she wasn't impressed. ***(Jack mimes explaining... demonstrates putting box on head)*** In fact she was furious. ***(grandmother stamps her foot)*** 'I've never heard such nonsense. In this life people and things wear out and there's nothing anyone can do about it,' she cried. Then she snatched the new-maker... ***(grandmother snatches new-maker)*** and hobbled off at top speed after the tramp to try and get their money back. ***(exit grandmother)***

Jack, meanwhile, sat down to enjoy his made-new cheese slice. ***(Jack sits down, takes cheese from pocket and peels back wrapper)*** But what was this? ***(Jack sniffs cheese)*** The cheese-slice didn't smell right. It definitely wasn't Granny's cheese. No, this was ordinary market cheese – the sort of cheese the tramp could have put inside the new-maker before he ever met Jack.

'Oh no! I've been tricked,' the boy gasped. ***(Jack throws away cheese slice in disgust)***

And with that, Granny came home. ***(enter grandmother with new-maker)*** 'The tramp tricked me,' cried Jack. 'His stupid new-maker doesn't work.' ***(takes box and throws it into the corner)***

'I know that,' said Granny kindly. ***(grandmother pats Jack's shoulder)*** 'I read the Book of Life every day and it stops me being taken in by false promises. It also reminds me of the things that never wear out – things inside us, like hope and love. Best of all it tells me that when my body *does* wear out, that's the beginning of a whole new story...

Granny would have gone on except there was a sudden burst of noise outside the door – the noise of a very excited *cow* ***(audience moo. Jack runs to door)***

'It's Daisy!' cried Jack. 'She's come home!'

Where Daisy had been neither Jack nor Granny ever found out. ***(Jack and grandmother scratch their heads and shrug)*** Of course rumour had it that a *cow...* ***(audience moo)*** had been spotted jumping over the moon... ***(grandmother mimes telling this to Jack)*** but Jack certainly wasn't about to fall for that one. ***(Jack laughs and shakes his head)*** Wherever she had been, Daisy's adventures didn't stop her giving plenty more milk. ***(Jack lifts bucket from under table, exits briefly and returns with it)*** Within a few days Granny was back making her smelly cheese. ***(grandmother sits at table and Jack turns round notice)*** And they all lived happily ever after.

APPLICATION

Theme: God makes things new

Explore: Paul's human weakness

Paul was human. His human body got tired and it seems he suffered from some sort of on-going illness which he called his 'thorn in the flesh' (2 Corinthians 12:7). He had two important things to say about this. First he said that every day God gave him new inner strength (2 Corinthians 4:16) and second he said that the human suffering wouldn't last long. Paul looked forward to 'a new heaven and a new earth' which God had promised (Isaiah 65:17). He knew that there he'd have a new body.

Chat

Share a snack together and chat about favourite foods. Make the point that things like food and sleep give us physical energy. Then ask what gives us spiritual energy? Help the children see that God wants to gives us new spiritual energy every day of our lives and, when our physical bodies wear out, he promises to renew them too.

Think

Thank God that the spiritual life he gives us never runs out.

DRAMA 49

A TALE OF TWO THRONES

AGE 11+

SUBJECT: **The Lordship of Christ**

BIBLE READING: **Philippians 2:6-11**

DRAMA NOTES: Suitable for group reading or performance.

Cast: Two narrators, Nero, mother, tutor, Christian, two guards (may be played by mother and tutor).
Staging: Opens with narrators side by side, stage left.
Throne centre stage.
Props: Chair to represent throne, scrolls, flip-flops (to fit Nero), scarf, guitars.

Narrator 1: In AD 54 a sixteen-year-old called Nero became the new Roman Emperor.

(enter Nero with his mother and tutor. Nero sits on the throne. His mother sits on the throne beside him)

Narrator 2: To begin with, it looked as if Nero would rule his empire well. ***(tutor shows scroll to Nero... Nero looks at it intently and nods... tutor smiles approvingly)*** He allowed himself to be guided by a wise tutor.

Narrator 1: And he shared power with his mother, Agrippina.

Narrator 2: But soon he'd had enough of that. ***(Nero pushes his mother off throne and waves goodbye. Mother flounces off)***

Narrator 1: Nero started to get bored. ***(tutor tries to show him another document. Nero waves it aside)***

Narrator 2: Suddenly, all he wanted was entertainment.

Narrator 1: Poetry, acting, dancing, horse-racing, music, girls... ***(Nero stands up, does a dance, mimes riding a horse, blows a kiss)***

Narrator 2: He started going around barefoot, with a scarf dangling round his neck, wearing what looked like a loose dressing gown. ***(Nero kicks off flip-flops, drapes a scarf round his neck. Enter Agrippina)***

Narrator 1: His mother was disgusted. ***(Agrippina stamps her foot and shakes her finger at Nero)***

Narrator 2: So Nero decided to have her killed. ***(Nero stamps his foot and turns his back, then swings round pointing at Agrippina, who doubles up and staggers off)***

Narrator 1: With Agrippina dead, Nero could really let his hair down. He'd always liked the sound of his own voice. ***(Nero grabs a guitar)***

Narrator 2: So now he launched his singing career. He gave concerts and held his audiences captive. ***(Nero mimes singing)***

Narrator 1: Literally.

Narrator 2: Nobody was allowed to leave the room while Nero sang.

Narrator 1: The story goes that women had babies during his performances and men escaped by pretending to die.

Narrator 2: In between concerts, Nero divorced his wife, Octavia and married his best friend's wife instead. ***(Nero sets guitar to one side and sits down on throne)***

Narrator 1: Then he had Octavia executed.

Narrator 2: And discovered he enjoyed having people killed even more than singing to them. ***(Nero rubs hands)***

Narrator 1: Nero's tutor got so fed up with his behaviour, he resigned. ***(tutor tries to get Nero to look at paper, Nero ignores him, tutor walks out)***

Narrator 2: Then in AD 64, a great fire broke out in Rome.

Narrator 1: The fire blazed for six whole days. ***(Nero picks up guitar again)***

Narrator 2: While the city burnt it is said that Nero climbed up into a tower and burst into song. ***(Nero stands on throne)*** Afterwards he blamed the fire on Christians.

Narrator 1: Which gave him a great excuse for killing them. ***(Christian is led on between two guards)***

Narrator 2: You could say killing Christians became his new hobby. ***(Nero mimes giving order)***

Narrator 1: He had them thrown to wild animals. ***(guards pretend to be animals attacking Christian)***

Narrator 2: Crucified. ***(guards pretend to nail Christian to cross)***

Narrator 1: Used as human torches and burned to death. ***(guards step back, shielding their faces as if Christian is ablaze)***

Narrator 2: He had around 5000 of them killed. ***(Nero steps down from throne and pretends to play guitar)***

Narrator 1: But of course that isn't the end of the story.

Narrator 2: For the Christians Nero persecuted had their own song.

Narrator 1: It was a song of faith. A song about Jesus dying on a cross… ***(Christian stretches out arms as if on a cross)*** being raised to the highest place in heaven… ***(Christian holds arms up to heaven)*** and reigning there until everyone knelt at his throne. ***(Christian kneels)***

Narrator 2: It was a song with more power packed into its few short lines than into all the Roman legions. A song that could never be silenced.

Narrator 1: Nero's voice was silenced.

Narrator 2: When he was 31, his legions turned against him. Knowing he was about to be flogged to death, he killed himself, leaving nothing but a nasty memory. ***(Nero mimes slitting his throat and staggers off stage)***

Narrator 2: But the memory of the lives of the Christians he killed inspired thousands to follow their example of faith. ***(guards kneel)***

Narrator 1: And that was just the beginning.

Narrator 2: By the time the Roman Empire fell apart, millions of people were living under the Lordship of Christ.

Narrator 1: And nearly two thousand years later, Christ's kingdom continues to spread throughout the earth.

Narrator 2: It is happening just as the song of faith promised: ***(narrators move centre stage and kneel)***

Narrator 1: 'At the name of Jesus everyone will bow -
those in heaven, on earth and under the earth

Narrator 2: and to the glory of God the Father
everyone will openly agree
'Jesus Christ is Lord.'

APPLICATION

Theme: Worshipping Christ as Lord

Explore: Philippians 2:6–11

The early Christians called the words of Philippians 2:6–11 the *Carmen Christi*, which is Latin for 'hymn to Christ'. The apostle Paul wrote the words of the song. Singing it strengthened the faith of the early Christians. It helped them remember who Jesus was, what he had done and what this meant.

Persecution

Persecution was a regular experience for the early Christians. This first Roman persecution under Nero (AD 64-68) was followed by nine more. You can read the story of Bishop Polycarp, one of the oldest Christian martyrs, in *50 Five Minute Stories,* published by Children's Ministry. Many other stories are to be found in *Jesus Freaks Vols I and II* by dc Talk and the *Voice of the Martyrs*.

Chat

Sing along with some praise songs which reflect the drama theme, e.g. 'You laid aside your majesty' *(CD: Children's Praise and Worship 4,* words and music in *250 Songs for Children's Praise and Worship*), 'We want to see Jesus lifted high' (CD: *Children's Praise and Worship 3*, words and music in *250 Songs for Children's Praise and Worship*), 'He is Lord' (words and music in *Songs of Fellowship vol.1*). Talk about the words of the songs and how they are saying similar things to the Carmen Christi. Jesus is enthroned in heaven and that his reign has already begun on earth even though lots of people don't realise it. Chat about the sort of power that is released in our lives when we worship Jesus as Lord.

Think

Ask children to think if they can sing 'He's *my* Lord' and really mean it?

DRAMA 50

KNOCK KNOCK

AGE 7+

SUBJECT: **Opening up to the Spirit**

BIBLE READING: **Revelation 3:20**

DRAMA NOTES: Suitable for performance or group reading. This is an interactive drama. Divide listeners into two groups. Group A growl when they hear the word **'wolf'**. Group B say 'swoosh' when they hear the word **'wind'**. The narrator should use a wood block to make a knocking sound every time the word **'knock'** or **'knocking'** appears in the script.

Cast: Narrator, wolf, pig.
Staging: Narrator stage left.
Props: Low table, armchair, stool, heavy coat, frying pan, cardboard knife, brush, apples, wood block.

Narrator: Pinky the Pig lived with Ed the **Wolf**. ***(enter wolf and pig)*** Pinky's house was always dark because Ed made her keep the curtains shut. ***(pig sits on stool. Wolf mimes shutting curtains)*** It was always cold because Ed wouldn't let Pinky light a fire. ***(pig shivers)*** And it smelt greasy because Ed made Pinky… ***(wolf hands pig frying pan)*** cook a big fry every day, with loads of bacon and sausage.

Still Ed was kind to Pinky – in a **wolfish** sort of way. ***(wolf puts arm round pig)*** He gave her a heavy fur coat to wear… ***(wolf gives pig coat)*** and lots of vegetables to eat. 'We need to fatten you up, little pig,' he'd say. 'I want to make you nice and plump and juicy.'

Then one day, as Pinky sat with Ed… ***(wolf sits in armchair, pig on stool)*** in her cold, dark, smelly home, she heard a **knock** at the door. ***(pig gets up)***

'Don't open it,' snarled the **wolf**. 'It's just the **wind**.' ***(pig sits down)***

The next day, at exactly the same time, the **knock** came again. ***(pig gets up)***

'Stay where you are. Don't move,' ***(pig sits down)*** snarled the **wolf**. 'Don't open that door to anyone – especially not the **wind**.' ***(wolf falls asleep)***

The next day when the **knock** came, Ed the **Wolf**, was asleep. ***(wolf snores)***

Timidly Pinky trotted to the door. ***(pig goes to door)*** 'Who's there?' she squeaked.

'It's the **wind**,' said a voice. 'Open the door and let me in.'

'Indeed I won't,' cried Pinky. ***(pig runs from door)*** 'Ed said I mustn't let anyone in – especially not the **wind**.'

'Little pig, if you want to save your bacon, you'll do as I ask,' said the voice.

'Don't you know what 'Ed' is short for?' ***(pig approaches door again)***

'Edward?' said Pinky.

'No,' said the voice. 'It's short for Wick-Ed.' ***(pig jumps with shock)***

'What's that? Who called my name?' the **wolf** woke up. ***(wolf wakes, pig runs from door)***

'It... it was the **wind**,' said Pinky. ***(pig cowers)***

'The **wind!**' roared the **wolf**. 'I told you. Have nothing to do with the **wind**. All the **wind** wants to do is come in like a hurricane and blow the house down.' ***(wolf whirls round mimicking a hurricane)***

Oh dear! Pinky didn't want to lose her house. So the next time the **knock** came to the door she stuck her trotters in her ears. ***(pig puts fingers in ears)***
Day after day the **wind** kept **knocking** and Pinky kept pretending not to hear… ***(pig puts fingers in ears)*** until one day the **wolf** snarled… ***(wolf jumps up)*** 'Bob the butcher is coming for a party and this house is a pig-sty. Clean it up.' ***(pig picks up brush)***

'Bob the butcher! Well I never!' Pinky started brushing the floor. ***(pig brushes floor)*** 'What will we give him to eat?'

(wolf picks up frying pan) 'A fry, of course,' said Ed. 'With lots of sausage and bacon.'

Pinky Pig looked in the larder. ***(pig pretends to look in cupboard)*** 'But we have no bacon and sausage left. It's all gone.'

'Don't you worry your piggy head about that,' smiled Ed. ***(wolf puts arm round pig)***

Pinky supposed Ed meant that Bob would bring bacon and sausage for the party tea.

'Am I invited?' she asked hopefully.

'You certainly are,' The **wolf** took a big carving knife from the drawer. ***(wolf picks up cardboard knife)*** 'There wouldn't be any party at all without you.'

As the **wolf** spoke, the **knocking** on the door came louder than ever, though Ed was too busy sharpening his knife to hear. ***(wolf sharpens knife. Pig moves to door)***

'Little pig, little pig, let me in,' cried the **wind**. 'You are in great danger.'

'No, I'm not,' cried Pinky. ***(pig shakes head)***

'Yes, you are,' cried the **wind**. 'Wicked **wolf** plans for Bob the butcher to turn you into bacon and sausage. He's sharpening that knife to cut your throat.'

'Come to me my little feast… I mean my little beast,' Ed called. ***(wolf beckons pig, licking lips)***

And in that instant Pinky made her choice.

'No! Come in, **wind**,' she cried.

And she flung open the door. ***(pig mimes opening door)*** Whoosh! Next thing Pinky knew, the **wind** was swirling round the room, blowing everything everywhere. ***(pig throws off her heavy coat. Wolf whirls round the stage and then exits)*** It blew open the curtains, it blew off her heavy fur coat and it picked up the **wolf** and tossed him, howling, up the chimney. Pinky ***(pig crouches behind table)*** expected that at any moment the house would blow down.

But it didn't. Instead the **wind** swooshed out into the garden and blew in a dozen rosy red apples. ***(apples roll on stage)***

'Come on, Pinky,' cried the **wind.** 'You must be hungry. Pick up the apples and bring them to the table.'

And suddenly Pinky realised how wonderfully different life was. ***(pig comes out and picks up apples)*** The **wolf** was gone and the **wind** had filled her house with sunlight. For the first time ever she was safe and warm and free. ***(pig sits down at table and bites into apple)***

APPLICATION

Theme: Opening our lives to the Spirit

Explore: The Book of Revelation

Revelation is the last book of the Bible. It was written around thirty years after Paul's missionary journeys, by one of Jesus' disciples – the apostle John. At the time when John was writing, the early Christians were suffering persecution under the Romans. The words given to John helped to strengthen their faith by showing them that Satan would one day be completely defeated.

Chat

Talk about bedrooms. Ask children to describe their bedrooms. Who shares a room with a brother or sister? Do they expect people to knock before coming into their room? How would they feel if someone came and sat down on their bed uninvited? Bring out the point that God's Holy Spirit never comes into anybody's life by force. Chat about how we open our lives to the Spirit.

Think

Think about bad habits and how a bad habit can be a bit like the wolf in today's drama, making us do the wrong thing. Praise God that the Holy Spirit has the power to set us free to live life to the full.

SUBJECT INDEX A–Z

Drama Number

SCRIPTURE INDEX